Collins need to know?

DIY

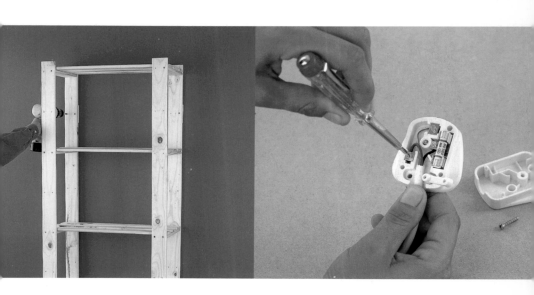

All the techniques, tools and tips
you need to do the job yourself

First published in 2005 by
Collins, an imprint of
HarperCollins*Publishers*
77–85 Fulham Palace Road
Hammersmith, London W6 8JB

The Collins website address is:
www.collins.co.uk

Collins is a registered trademark of HarperCollins Publishers Limited

08 07 06 05
6 5 4 3 2 1

Based on material from *DIY Survival* by Tommy Walsh
Photography by Tim Ridley

A catalogue record for this book is available from the British Library

Created by: **Focus Publishing**, Sevenoaks, Kent
Project editor: Guy Croton
Editor: Vanessa Townsend
Designer: David Etherington
Project co-ordinator: Caroline Watson
Cover design: Cook Design
Front cover photograph: © Getty Images/Michael Wildsmith

ISBN 0 00 719447 1

Colour reproduction by Colourscan, Singapore
Printed and bound by Printing Express Ltd, Hong Kong

Please note: always take care when embarking on any DIY project. Read the instructions for tools before you commence and take appropriate safety precautions. Great care has been taken to ensure that the information contained in this book is accurate and correct. However, the publishers can accept no responsibility or liability for any loss or damage.

Regulations to protect consumers from dangerous electrical workmanship now exist. Part P of the building regulations states that all domestic electrical installations (with the exception of minor work) must be installed, or inspected and certified, by a 'competent person', or the homeowner is required to inform their local authority building control (LABC) department, which will inspect the work.

It is the reader's responsibility to ensure that their proposed electrical project complies with Part P of the building regulations before commencing electrical work of any kind. The publishers accept no liability for any loss, damage or injury arising from the reader's failure to do so.

For details of these regulations and for a definition of 'minor work', which is excepted from the rules, please visit www.partp.co.uk and www.odpm.gov.uk.

Ignoring the regulations is a criminal offence.

contents

basics

Good quality DIY depends upon sound preparation, the use of the right tools and a methodical, unhurried approach to the job in hand. Get the basics right, and the rest will often follow naturally from there. If you are new to DIY, read on...

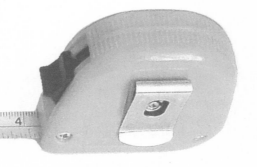

▶ Tools

There is no DIY without tools. Always buy the best ones you can afford, as cheap tools can be frustrating or even dangerous to use. Also, make sure you select the right tool for the job.

General tools

Many tools have multiple purposes, which makes them especially useful. Most of the tools featured on these pages fall into this category. As well as good general tools, a sturdy tool box is a wise investment: you will be able to protect your tools and keep them well organised, so that you know exactly where to find a particular item when you need it.

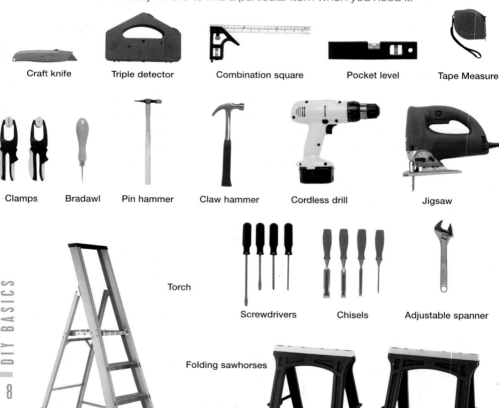

Craft knife   Triple detector   Combination square   Pocket level   Tape Measure

Clamps   Bradawl   Pin hammer   Claw hammer   Cordless drill   Jigsaw

Torch   Screwdrivers   Chisels   Adjustable spanner

Folding sawhorses

Step ladder

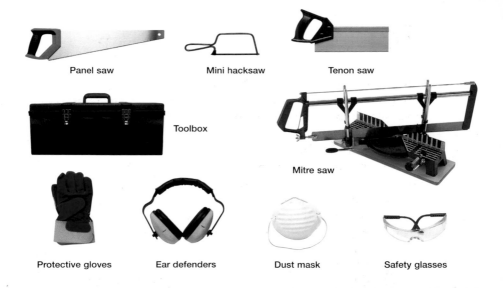

Panel saw

Mini hacksaw

Tenon saw

Toolbox

Mitre saw

Protective gloves

Ear defenders

Dust mask

Safety glasses

Plumbing tools

You should only need many of the tools featured in this section if you get a blockage somewhere in your plumbing system. However, the wrenches are handy for holding pipe work or undoing nuts on taps. Also, the radiator key is an invaluable little tool for curing knocks, splutters and bangs in your heating system, so always keep one of these handy.

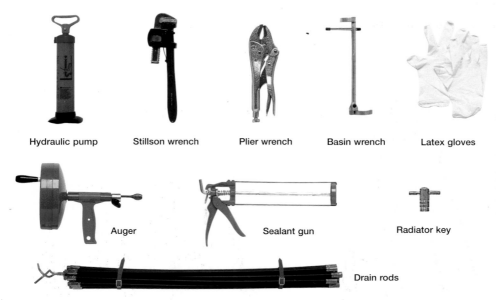

Hydraulic pump

Stillson wrench

Plier wrench

Basin wrench

Latex gloves

Auger

Sealant gun

Radiator key

Drain rods

Electrical tools

Not surprisingly, many people find the thought of working with electricity very daunting. It is dangerous and needs to be treated with the utmost respect – even the simple repairs covered in this book require care and attention. Having said that, these few basic tools will help you with most jobs, and you don't necessarily need all of them. You'll find detailed descriptions of what they all do in the electrical projects.

WATCH OUT!

Shocking news
Electricity is responsible for more DIY deaths than anything else, so treat it with respect and, if in doubt, just don't do it.

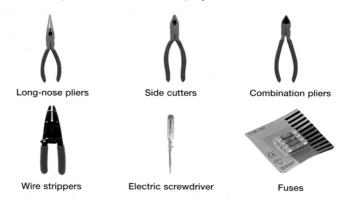

Long-nose pliers   Side cutters   Combination pliers

Wire strippers   Electric screwdriver   Fuses

Decorating tools

As is the case with most tools, the more money you spend on decorating tools, the better they will perform the job in hand. This is especially true of paint brushes: cheap brushes which moult bristles are incredibly frustrating to use and can literally ruin an entire decorating job. A tile cutter (see opposite) is a good investment – it will save a lot of time and energy and will make a neat job of cutting bathroom and kitchen tiles.

Paint brushes   Roller and tray   Scissors   Sponge

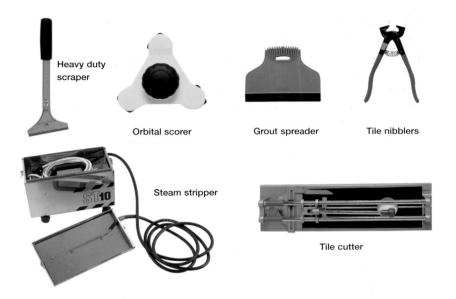

Heavy duty scraper

Orbital scorer

Grout spreader

Tile nibblers

Steam stripper

Tile cutter

Exterior tools

There are not many additional tools needed for exterior work. Many of those you will require are already covered under 'general tools' on page 8. However, a spirit level is always a vital piece of equipment, as is a sturdy bucket – though you will probably find plenty of uses for these throughout this book, both indoors and out! While a sledgehammer will help you dismantle walls or paving, the trowels and rubber mallet are good for reconstruction work or building from scratch. Finally, any drilling into an exterior wall will require a sturdy masonry bit (see page 13).

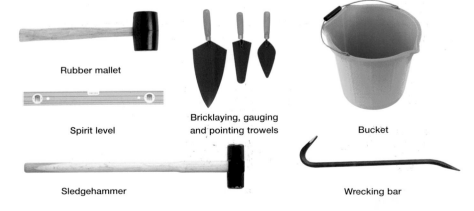

Rubber mallet

Spirit level

Bricklaying, gauging and pointing trowels

Bucket

Sledgehammer

Wrecking bar

Basic fixings

If tools are what facilitate successful DIY, then fixings are what hold it all together. It does not matter how skilfully you wield your hammer, screwdriver or drill – if you do not use the right fixing in the right way, your DIY project will fail and could be a source of irritation for months to come.

Getting something to stay where you want it may be more difficult than you think. Even drilling a hole will require some planning. For example, not only do you need to know exactly where the hole should be, but you should also know what type of fixing you will be using and what type of drill bit you need for that surface.

Basically, nails are fine for holding things together temporarily, but screws are best for permanent fixings and anything that requires in-built strength. Screws come with either cross heads or slotted heads, in a range of gauges and sizes. If you need to fix into a wall, then wall plugs will be essential. The wall plug goes into the drilled hole, and then holds the screw securely in the wall as you drive it into the plug.

Depending on the job in hand, you will need a variety of drill bits. There are wood bits, HSS bits which are designed for drilling through metal, and masonry bits for drilling through masonry, stone and brickwork.

Duct tape is waterproof, highly adhesive and very handy for all kinds of jobs. You can use masking tape to mask off the edges of areas that you want to paint, while electrical tape is useful for insulating and securing flex.

Finally, there are many types of glue and adhesive available, but you cannot go too far wrong with the few basic ones shown here. Remember that sealant is just that – it is for sealing, and is not an alternative to glue.

MUST KNOW

The right stuff
Always use the correct fixing for the task in hand. Do not be tempted to use a nail when a screw is required, or a tack when glue will do the job more effectively. The golden rule of DIY is better safe than sorry: economising or being lazy about what you need may seem like a good idea at the time, but wait until your job falls apart...

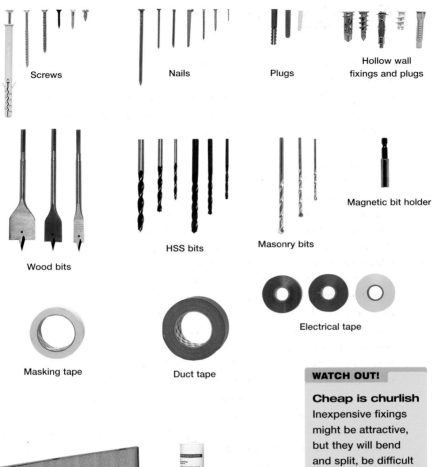

Screws

Nails

Plugs

Hollow wall fixings and plugs

Wood bits

HSS bits

Masonry bits

Magnetic bit holder

Masking tape

Duct tape

Electrical tape

Sealant

Multipurpose adhesive

Fixings box

Wood glue

Routine checks

Although DIY is often about fun projects and building things from scratch, there is also a more mundane side to taking care of your own property. This entails checking that everything is working properly on a regular basis – from the plumbing and heating systems to basic household electrics.

One of the most potentially damaging problems that can occur in a house is a burst or damaged water pipe. Unnoticed, one of these can cause a huge amount of damage and inconvenience, particularly during the winter months, when pipes are often subjected to the extremes of cold weather. Problems will frequently occur when the occupants are away on holiday, even for a couple of days, and prevention rather than cure is the obvious answer. So turn off the water supply when you go away! This means that you must locate the water supply stopcock.

For a house, there is normally a stopcock in the front garden near the boundary or outside the property boundary in the street. This stopcock is the property of the water authority. However, any leaks that occur on the property side of the stopcock are the responsibility of the householder. The stopcock can usually be accessed by a turnkey, which can be purchased from a plumber's or builder's merchant. Turning off from here will automatically cut the supply to your house.

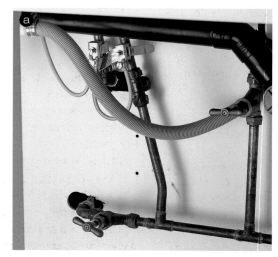

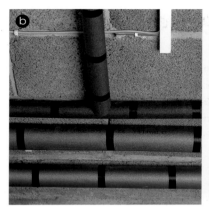

Houses and flats normally have a stopcock inside the building close to the first call on the supply. This will typically be the kitchen sink for fresh drinking water and the stopcock is commonly positioned under the sink or nearby [a]. Turning off this stopcock will isolate the incoming supply. A water supply normally diverts after the kitchen sink and feeds a storage tank in the loft or cupboard, which in turn supplies the bath, WC and hand basin with the coldwater supply. This water is not for drinking.

The supply feed pipe to the tank also has a stopcock to enable you to isolate the supply to the bathroom area without stopping the freshwater supply to your kitchen sink.

In an emergency, shut off all stopcocks and empty the water storage tank by turning on the bath and hand basin cold taps and repeatedly flushing the toilet. This will empty the system down the drains and will prevent your house from flooding.

Check whether your water pipes and storage tank are lagged [b]. Lagging is not expensive and could save you a fortune in heating bills and split, frozen pipes in the long term.

The second power source you need to locate is the mains gas shut off valve [c]. The valve is

DIY BASICS

15

normally located on the incoming supply just before the meter. It requires just a quarter turn off and on. Again, the valve is normally located in a cupboard under the stairs or in a high position in an accessible area such as a first-floor landing. In recent years, gas supply companies have been fitting the supply meters and valves to an outside box. This is often the case in properties that have been divided into flats.

Another important routine check is to establish what type of boiler system you have. A family or very large house would normally have a conventional system, which incorporates a gas boiler **[d]** and copper cylinder **[e]**. In smaller properties, gas combination boiler systems are commonly used, which will only heat the water as you require it and do not feature a cylinder storage system. Carefully read all instructions on how to start the boiler and how to operate the timer switches. Additionally, you should keep a written record next to the boiler indicating when the previous services were made and when future services are required. Servicing of the appliance is very important to ensure that the boiler is running correctly and that no toxic emissions are returning into the property. Make sure that ANY

gas work undertaken in your property, is carried out by a CORGI-registered contractor – and check his credentials.

Another vital piece of equipment to locate in your home is the electricity supply fuse board, commonly known as a consumer unit **[f]**. The consumer unit will generally be positioned in a cupboard, possibly under the stairs, or high up by the front door, and controls the electrical supply to your home **[g]**. Inspect the unit and check what type of fuses it contains to see whether they are the old fuse wire type or more recent cartridges, and make sure that you always have some spares close at hand. It is a good idea to keep a torch, electrical screwdriver and a pack of assorted fuse wire next to the consumer unit, as well as candles and matches as a back up, in case the batteries in the torch should run flat.

Finally, keep a list of important emergency numbers to hand of key tradesmen such as plumbers, electricians and boiler repair men **[h]**. If possible, list the contact details of at least two of each, to guard against absences at important times. Above all, make sure that all your essential household systems are serviced regularly – prevention is always better than cure.

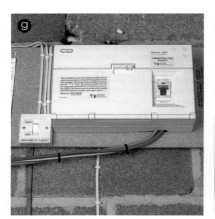

g

h

Planning the job

Being well organised and planning a detailed *modus operandi* are hallmarks of the successful DIY-er. You should never embark on a job without a clear idea of how it will be accomplished.

It is essential to plan any DIY job carefully. A written plan is always advisable **[a]**, as there are always so many factors to bear in mind. Should you cover the carpets with sheets or roll them up? If you can, roll them up. No matter how careful you are, you are bound to knock over a can of paint or a bucket of paste, so decant the contents of larger containers into smaller ones to reduce the likelihood of mishaps **[b]**.

MUST KNOW

First aid

If you plan your DIY jobs properly and always take your time, with a bit of luck you won't need a first aid kit. However, there is an element of risk with many jobs, and it is just as well to be prepared, so keep a good basic kit to hand in case of emergencies. In addition to the items listed below, make sure you include some antiseptic cream and some eyewash. You can buy ready-made up kits in most DIY stores, chemists or department stores. Remember always to replace items if and when you use them.

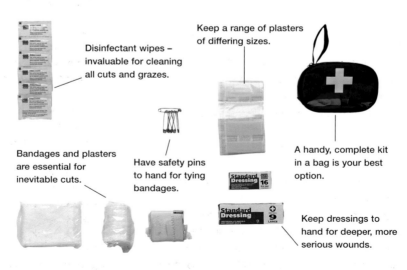

Disinfectant wipes – invaluable for cleaning all cuts and grazes.

Keep a range of plasters of differing sizes.

A handy, complete kit in a bag is your best option.

Bandages and plasters are essential for inevitable cuts.

Have safety pins to hand for tying bandages.

Keep dressings to hand for deeper, more serious wounds.

Standard Dressing 16

Standard Dressing 9

Will you be stripping paper from the walls? Then hire or buy a wallpaper steam stripper; it will save you time and money. If you are decorating, there's also sanding down the woodwork, painting the ceiling, painting the woodwork, to consider – the list is endless.

Do not be tempted to rush the job. Prepare and strip the walls in one weekend, then purchase the materials and complete the job the following weekend. As a result, your project will be pleasant and rewarding, and will feel a lot less like a chore. Use the time you save to plan the next job on the list or to clear up earlier efforts properly.

When possible, always try to carry out DIY tasks in daylight hours. Use the evenings for planning and get an early start on the job. In terms of what you can achieve, the hours between 7am and midday are worth twice as much as the hours between noon and 6pm.

If you need to sand down furniture or moveable objects, try to do the job outside. If that is not possible, or you are sanding fixed floors, seal the door of the room with masking tape and polythene, and then cover everything with a dustsheet. Open the windows and wear a mask. Also, if the work you are planning will be noisy, try to keep your neighbours in mind; call and tell them what you intend to do and remember to finish at a reasonable hour.

In your planning stage, always make sure that you allow for protective coverings and cleaning equipment such as: dustsheets; polythene; heavy duty rubbish bags; cleaning rags; brush and pan; mop and bucket; disinfectant and air fresheners. Also, have to hand a first aid kit (see box, opposite), and, most importantly, don't forget to include all the health and safety gear that you will need.

want to know more?

Take it to the next level...

Go to...
▶ **Preparation** – pages 24–7
▶ **Hanging pictures** – pages 48–9
▶ **Sanding floors** – pages 86–7

Other sources
▶ **DIY courses**
  check with your local authority for adult evening classes
▶ **Local DIY stores**
  can usually offer plenty of advice if you are unsure about tackling a job
▶ **Internet**
  visit www.diyfixit.co.uk
▶ **Books**
  Collins Complete DIY Manual

painting &

decorating

Many people who are new to DIY begin by trying some painting and decorating. While it is fair to say that this is one of the more straightforward areas of the hobby, it is a mistake to think that good decorating is easy. On the contrary, there is much to learn!

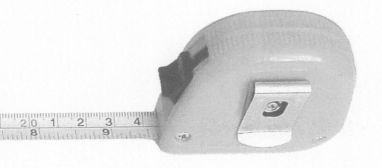

Stripping walls and ceilings

In order to get a decent result from painting or applying new paper to a wall, it is vital first to strip away old wallpaper, ceramic tiles or any other wall covering.

Stripping wallpaper

Before you actually begin stripping your walls, remove the carpets and underlay, roll them up, tie them with string and store them away. Score the walls all over with the edge of your scraper or a wallpaper scorer **[a]**, and soak the paper with warm soapy water and a sponge. Work a rotation system on the walls – in between stripping one, keep soaking the other in preparation.

Ceilings are a lot more difficult to strip, depending on what paint has been used over the paper. It is a good idea either to buy or hire a steam stripper as they are also useful for walls **[b]**. When using a steam stripper, follow the instructions carefully and adhere to the safety advice. Don't hold the steamer in one place for too long or you may loosen the plaster finish coat on old walls. Well-soaked wallpaper should

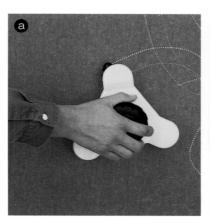

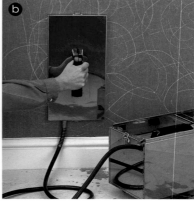

practically fall off. A lot of plaster damage can occur by using the scraper forcefully on paper that has not been soaked through thoroughly **[c]**. If in doubt, peel the paper off by hand.

When stripping wallpaper directly above a socket or light switch, turn off the power supply temporarily, and loosen off the socket and switch faces, to allow for the paper to be completely removed. Make sure sockets are dry before switching the power back on.

To remove any backing paper, soak with warm, slightly soapy water applied with a paddle brush. Apply at least two soakings, allowing approximately 20 minutes to soak through. When all the paper is removed from the walls with a scraper **[d]**, dispose of all the waste and wash the walls down with a warm water and mild detergent solution.

Removing ceramic tiles

Goggles and gloves are essential when removing tiles, as sharp splinters can fly away and cut easily. Use the bolster chisel to break out one tile initially. This will allow you to get the bolster chisel behind the next tile more easily. Use the bolster and hammer to remove the old adhesive. Clean the walls and clear the floor as you go.

▲ Use a hammer and bolster to strip away old ceramic tiles. Watch out for flying chips.

MUST KNOW

Stripping ceilings
This is not a straightforward task and it is essential to use a steam stripper. Most importantly, set up a safe platform to work from – don't just use a stepladder!

Preparing walls & ceilings for decoration

There is an old saying in DIY circles which states that any job is only ever as good as the preparation that went into it. Nowhere is this more true than in the case of preparing walls and ceilings for decoration. Once you have stripped away old wallcoverings, it is then essential to make good any old and rotting plaster before starting to decorate.

If you rush the preparation work prior to decorating, once the job is done every time you walk in the room, the bits that you are not happy with will stand out so much to you that it will drive you crazy. So, always take your time and prepare properly! Even the roughest of walls can be immensely improved with painstaking preparation.

Your decorating kit, which ought to be of the best quality you can afford, should feature at least a couple of filling knives, both broad and narrow bladed. These useful tools look exactly the same as scrapers, but are much more flexible, enabling the filling of damaged walls to be carried out much more effectively than if you used a scraper.

Often in older properties, when the paper is removed, areas of finish plaster (the top coat) come away from the base coat. Ensure that the topcoat edges are stable, but do not insert your scraper under the finish or you will inadvertently remove more and more of the surface. When you are dealing with plaster damage, always cut and scrape towards the centre of the damaged area from the sides. Prepare the entire wall, and apply a solution of PVA adhesive and water to the dry damaged areas with a paintbrush. Prepare and mix your filler by adding water to

MUST KNOW

Tools required

Scrapers
Filler knifes
Sponge
Mastic gun
Mastic
Hammer
Batten
Sandpaper
Craft knife

Close scrapes

When scraping paper off walls or sanding down old plaster or new filler, it is a good idea to wear gloves. This is because it can be just as easy to scrape your knuckles as it is the wall!

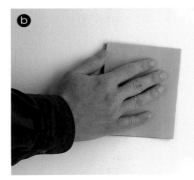

the powder, and then gently apply it to the damaged sections. In areas of cracked plaster, cut out the crack to form a 'V' shape using the corner of the scraper. Apply the PVA and water solution, and fill with the knife **[a]**. Wait for the filler to dry and then sand it down using fine grade paper. Fold the paper and rub lightly over the filled surface until it is smooth **[b]**.

The corners of walls often get damaged, as they are far more vulnerable to being knocked. Pinning a temporary batten to the wall and filling in the gaps will easily rectify this common problem **[c]**.

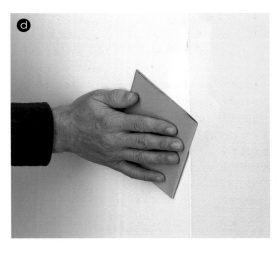

Leave the filler overnight to cure properly, then remove the batten and fill in the pinholes. When the filler is completely dry, sand the surface smooth, as before **[d]**.

When you have completed the sanding down of the filler and swept up or vacuumed the dust, use clean water and a sponge to rinse over the walls in order to remove any residue or debris prior to redecorating **[e]**.

There are lots of new decorating aids available on the market today. One of these, decorator's caulk, is particularly useful. This is mastic in a tube, which you apply with a mastic gun. When you purchase mastic, ensure that you buy the right one for the job. There is a wide range available to do a variety of jobs. For decorating, you need a water-soluble decorator's caulk (NOT silicone). This caulk is wonderful for flexible filling between the walls and skirtings or around door and window architraves. You may find you have different size cracks to fill, so start by cutting off just the tip of the caulk nozzle applicator with a craft knife and fill all the narrow cracks **[f]**. For broader cracks, cut off more of the nozzle to create a wider bead.

Smooth mastic

Getting a really good finish on a bead of mastic can be extremely difficult without lots of regular practice. However, running the back of a moist teaspoon along the bead can help to smooth out any lumps or inconsistencies – but use one that isn't for stirring your tea!

Using a mastic gun effectively takes a bit of practice. It is best to start at the top and then, making a smooth flowing motion, apply the bead in a steady line along the crack **[g]**. Remember to release the trigger to cut off the mastic flow at the end of the run, to prevent oozing.

Smooth off the caulk with a damp sponge **[h]**, regularly rinsing out the sponge to avoid any mess. Use the sponge very gently, as it is important not to spoil the finish of the bead by ruffling it. Any imperfections will be even more noticeable once the caulk has dried.

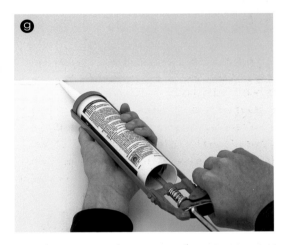

Painting walls and ceilings

Once you have completed your preparations – and allowed all filler and other materials to dry out thoroughly – it is at last time to embark on the more fulfilling part of the job. Ensure that you have everything you need to hand before you start painting, as juggling with rollers and brushes later on is not advisable.

When painting ceilings, the best method is to use a lambswool roller **[a]**. If possible, fit an extension pole to enable you to reach the ceiling comfortably from the floor, but if this isn't possible, set up a safe, sturdy work platform. Remember to cover the floor with dustsheets or newspaper and use the roller slowly across the ceiling, or more paint will end up on the floor than on the ceiling. The roller will only take the paint close to the walls. The edges of the ceiling will need to be painted using a brush **[b]**. This brushwork is known as 'cutting in'. If the paint overlaps onto the walls a bit, it doesn't matter, as the wall colour will cover that overlap when it

a

is applied. If the room features a coving or a cornice, this should be painted in the same colour as the ceiling – unless you wish to make it stand out in its own colour.

When painting walls, again the best method is to use a roller – not too vigorously, or the paint will splash onto the woodwork and the newly painted ceiling. Using the roller, cover the walls with the paint **[c]**. The parts that cannot be

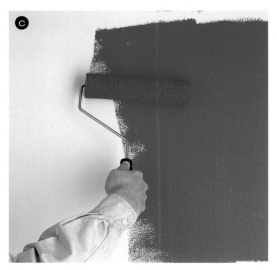

Tools required
Dust sheets
Roller
Roller tray
Brushes
Stepladder
Platform
Radiator roller
Cling film

reached with the roller will need to be completed with a brush. Splashes of paint on the woodwork or walls should be removed with a damp sponge or cloth while they are still wet.

Using a brush and cutting in at ceiling level requires a steady hand **[d]**, as otherwise it is easy to make a mess with the paint and leave a wavy edge to both the ceiling and the adjacent wall. For this reason, make sure that you are

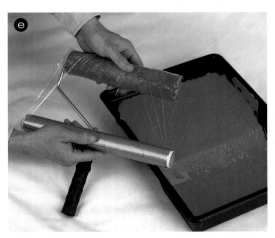

positioned as comfortably as possible before embarking on the cutting in, especially if you have to stand at the top of a stepladder. Also, choose a time when you are fresh and at your best; it is not a good idea to undertake this tricky part of the job when

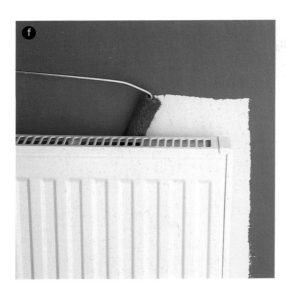

WATCH OUT!

Wait until it's dry...

Do not be tempted to use a different colour or type of paint on an adjacent wall or feature before other nearby paint has fully dried. For example, it is not a good idea to begin painting a radiator with white gloss paint while the different-coloured emulsion on the wall behind it is still wet. It is all too easy for the paints to run together and make a mess.

you are feeling tired or at all unsteady, perhaps at the end of a long hard day of decorating.

If you have to pop out or take a break in between applying coats of paint, you can wrap your roller and brushes in cling film to prevent them from going stiff and crusty before you have finished using them **[e]**.

Every decorating job involves an awkward corner or inaccessible part of the room. For example, there is always the tricky space behind the radiator that needs doing. If you don't want to put up with the inconvenience of having to remove the radiator, then simply use a slim, extended radiator roller to reach as far down or up as you need to go **[f]**.

One important consideration when decorating is to ensure that any ladders or platforms are safely constructed and positioned. Stairwells present particular problems in this regard, as they are such an awkward shape and of a dangerous depth, but tailor-made platforms for these areas are available to hire, or with care you can build your own.

MUST KNOW

High rollers

Sheepskin rollers tend not to have very long lives. Even those of the best quality soon start to moult and lose their pliancy, which reduces their efficiency. However, you do not need to replace the entire roller every time; simply buy a replacement sheepskin sleeve.

PAINTING & DECORATING

31

Varnishing & painting windows & doors

Doors and windows present special challenges to the amateur decorator, requiring different preparation prior to painting and a whole set of new techniques during the job.

Varnishing doors & windows

There are many different types of wood varnish, but all need to be applied in the same fashion to achieve a perfect finish.

Your door or window will need to be prepared thoroughly as for painting. If you have bare wood, this should be brushed free of any particles.

Thin the first coat of varnish by 10 per cent to form a sealer coat. Apply the sealer using a brush **[a]**. Always apply varnish in the direction of the wood grain and allow enough time in between coats for the varnish to dry in accordance with the manufacturer's instructions.

Lightly key the surface with the fine flour sandpaper in between coats **[b]**, and then, using a cloth and white spirit, clean the surface and apply a full coat of varnish. Apply a third coat for a really perfect finish.

MUST KNOW

Tools required
Brushes – medium, fine
Flour sandpaper
White spirit
Cloth
Window scraper
Paint stripper
Mask
Safety glasses
Protective gloves

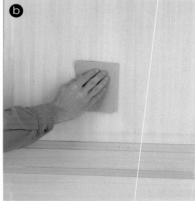

Painting doors

Preparation is all-important when painting doors. Remove all the door furniture (and keep the handle in the room with you, just in case). If painting on bare wood, any knots should be treated with knot solution and the door primed. If you are painting the door different colours inside and out, paint the outer edge of the door the same colour as the inside opening face, with each frame matching the closing face of the door.

If you are painting a flush door, start at the top and use a mini roller, working down in vertical sections blending one into the other **[c]**. Lay on the paint, then finish each vertical section with light strokes. Finally, paint the edges using a 25mm (1in) brush to avoid any paint seams running down the door **[d]**.

Painting windows

When painting windows, you will first need to remove the levers, catches and stays and then keep the window open using some stiff wire looped around a nail driven into the underside of the open casement and hooked into one of the screw holes on the frame. Clean the glass before painting the window.

Prepare the surface by sanding and wipe away any residue. Paint the outside of the casement first, always starting on the innermost edge and moving to the outer surfaces. Follow up by painting the fixed window frame from the beading or putty surface, then moving to the face of the frame. You can either mask the edge of your windows with masking tape to avoid getting paint on the windows, or remove any overspill with a window scraper afterwards. Remember, for all painting, use the first third of the brush. Do not overload the brush with paint **[e]**.

▶ Hanging wallpaper

The discipline of hanging wallpaper has been the stock in trade of jokes about DIY for many years. This is because it can be full of pitfalls unless undertaken properly and with care.

If you are right handed, you will find it easiest to start at the left of the door and work your way around the room – from right to left. An alternative method is to start between two windows, or the centre of a chimneybreast, particularly if the paper has a large and impressive pattern. Then you should ensure that, upon entering the room, the prominent focal point your eyes find is the position that you set the paper out from.

Once you have decided on your starting position, the first thing to do is to mark a vertical level line on the wall using either a plumb line and bob, or a long spirit level, rotating the level as you mark.

Hold the end of the wallpaper up to the ceiling **[a]**. Allow surplus paper for trimming, both top and bottom. Pre-cut enough lengths to cover at least one wall. Check to make sure you have allowed enough paper to enable a match on well spaced repeating patterns. These lengths of paper are known as 'drops'.

Roll out all the drops that you have pre-cut face down on a pasting table ready for pasting. Cover the whole table surface (so no paste gets onto the face of the paper). Apply the paste using a large pasting brush, pasting away from the centre. Fold the pasted paper in a concertina shape paste-to-paste, and face-to-face. Set

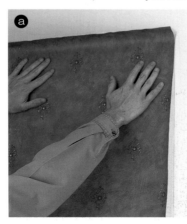

a

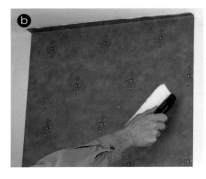

aside the drops to soak and apply a coat of watery paste to the walls. This technique is called sizing, and will make hanging the paper much easier. It also prevents the plaster from soaking up the paste from the paper.

Hold the first pasted drop up to the ceiling and manoeuvre the drop parallel to the marked line, allowing for trimming. Carefully brush from the centre of the paper out towards the edges, expelling any trapped air bubbles **[b]**. Continue this procedure along the whole length of the drop. Using a thin straight edge, tuck the paper tightly into the ceiling joint and trim with a very sharp craft knife **[c]**. Repeat this process at skirting level.

Repeat the process with the other drops, ensuring that the pattern matches and the edges butt, as you brush out any air bubbles **[d]**. Use a damp sponge to sponge off any excess paste to the paper and ceiling **[e]**.

MUST KNOW

Tools required
Pasting bench
Paste brush
Craft knife
Seam roller
Paper shears
Paper brush
Sponge
Oilstone
Plumb bob
Spirit level

PAINTING & DECORATING

Fixing wall tiles

Tiling is not as difficult a job as many people fear, but done badly it can be a very expensive mistake and can look terrible. The key thing is to take your time and remain patient. Also, make sure that you have plenty of spare tiles from the outset, as cutting tiles can be a hit-and-miss affair.

Begin by taking a length of batten approximately 1900mm (6ft 3in) long. Carefully lay out some of your tiles with spacers, marking the batten to create a gauging rod. Offer the rod up to the wall to determine where to start and to keep the cuts at the top, bottom and both corners of the room as equal as you possibly can.

Once you have established your ideal starting position, fix a full horizontal batten above the skirting board at that point, using a spirit level. Also fix a vertical batten near the corner of the room. Drill and fix these battens with screws and plugs **[a]**. The battens define the area you are going to tile and act as straight-edged guides throughout the process.

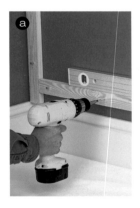

Using a serrated trowel or spreader, apply tile adhesive evenly over the wall, covering no more than approximately a square metre at a time **[b]**. Wall tile adhesive usually comes pre-mixed in large tubs. Press the tiles firmly into the

adhesive, remembering to insert the spacers between the tiles as you go. Once all the full tiles are fixed, remove the battens **[c]** ready to prepare and place cut tiles all around the edges.

Cutting tiles is best and fairly effortlessly carried out using a hand operated tile cutter. To mark a tile for cutting, hold it face down into the corner and mark with a felt tip pen, allowing for spacers. Cut the tile **[d]**. Spread the adhesive on the back of the cut tile and place it carefully in position.

Many tile adhesives can also be used as grout or it can be purchased in powder form and made into a creamy paste by adding water. The best method of application is to use a rubber-grouting float (a wooden handled float with a rubber face), which allows you to push the grout around into all the joints easily **[e]**.

It is important to remove all the excess grout from the surface of the tiles before it hardens. Use a bucket of clean water and a damp sponge. To finish off, polish the tiles with a dry cloth.

To finish the job and improve the look of the grout, rub the lines between the tiles over with a jointer to compress and smooth over the joints **[f]**. You can buy jointers or simply shape a piece of wood or plastic to make a perfectly good tool. Finally, polish the tiles once more with a dry cloth.

MUST KNOW

Tools required
Tile nibblers
Gauge stick
Spirit level
Pencil
Drill
Screws and plugs
Serrated spreader
Rubber spreader
Tile cutter
Felt-tip pen
Clean cloth

Installing cornice and coving

Cornices and coving bring an extra dimension to rooms, which can look bare without them. They are widely available ready-made and not difficult to cut and fit.

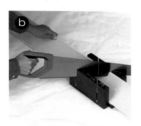

Fitting coving

Cut a short length of cove or cornice, offer it up and mark the position that the finished coving will occupy on the walls and ceilings in every corner of the room **[a]**. Using a chalk line, pin one end onto a mark and stretch a line tautly to the other mark. Carefully snap the line to leave the chalk marks around the whole room. Rub the finish plaster within the marked lines with the edge of a scraper in order to create a key for the adhesive. Next, apply a solution of PVA adhesive and water to the prepared surface. This will prevent the plaster from sucking the water from the adhesive and generally helps with adhesion.

A paper template is usually provided with the ready-made coving to enable you to cut the internal and external mitre joints that are required to allow the coving to butt together in corners. An easier way to cut a mitre is by using a big mitre block, which you can buy **[b]** or very easily make. Four different mitres are required – left and right internal, and left and right external.

The fixing adhesive is normally supplied in bags of dry powder, which you simply add to water and mix. To make mixing quicker and easier, a mixing tool can be purchased from a DIY store to fit into your electric drill. Use the slow speed on the drill, so as not to make mess **[c]**. The mixture should have the consistency of clotted cream and should be applied with either a pointing trowel or a filling knife **[d]**.

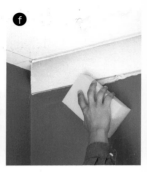

Cutting good mitres takes practice and experience. However, do not worry if your mitre cuts are not perfect, because the coving joints can easily be filled and shaped with some of the excess adhesive. However, on a cornice the joints would have to be over-filled with casting plaster when set, and the pattern cut out with a special weapon called a 'trowel end small tool'. These come in a range of different shapes and sizes, but basically resemble a long steel drawer handle with a spoon shape at one end (for applying plaster) and a blade shape at the other end (for carving).

When pressing coving (or cornice) into position, the crucial guide to follow is the chalk line on the wall, because that is the line that the eye will see **[e]**. Quite often the ceilings are out of true, but you can pack any gaps with adhesive or filler and, when painted, it will not show. Consequently, do not try to force the coving or cornice to meet both surfaces: instead, keep it straight and fill any gaps.

Carefully scrape off the excess adhesive with a filling knife or trowel and then rub over with a damp sponge to remove all traces of excess adhesive and to leave a smooth finish **[f]**. Finally, as a temporary measure, hammer some nails into the wall immediately beneath the cove or cornice, as these will hold the coving or cornice in place while the adhesive dries **[g]**.

Fitting dado and picture rails

Dado and picture rails can give a room a lift and also offer added practicality as you can suspend items from them. Both types of rail are remarkably easy to fix to the walls.

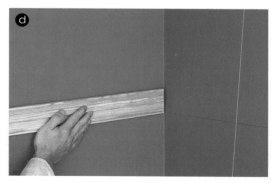

Mark the desired position of the dado rail on the walls. The height you select to fix the rail at is your choice, but it may look odd if it is much higher than a metre (3ft 3in) from the floor. Using a spirit level, rotating it as you go, draw a line around the room **[a]**. The height of a picture rail is usually about 300–500mm (1ft–1ft 8in) below the ceiling cornice. To cut a dado or picture rail to length, you will need a mitre block and tenon saw or a mitre saw **[b]**. When joining two pieces at a corner, mitre the ends to make a perfect 90° angle.

You can now buy special adhesives to fix timber features such as picture and dado rails. Just apply the adhesive with a sealant gun **[c]**, and press the rail into place **[d]**. In the case of a modern wall constructed from timber studwork (framework) and plasterboard, use 50–65mm (2–2½in) lost head nails through the rail fixed into the vertical studwork timbers. Knock the nails

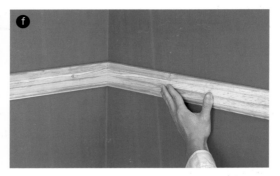

below the surface using a punch **[e]**. Fill the nail holes afterwards with proprietary filler.

If you are lucky, then the corners of your room might be nice and square. That would enable you to cut an internal mitre to fit the corners perfectly. Another way to cut two pieces for an internal corner, is to cut one piece square ended and fix it, then to scribe the second piece over the first. A scribe is obtained by first cutting an internal mitre. Using a coping saw, cut off the mitre leaving just the profile. This should then fit snugly over the first piece **[f]**. Two pieces of rail can be joined together by means of mitring on a 45° angle and fixing the first piece. Mitre the second piece to fit perfectly over the first, using a touch of PVA **[g]**. Add an extra bit of strength to an external corner by knocking in a pin or two **[h]**.

Creating a decorative wall panel effect

Another way of easily brightening up your walls and making your living room more interesting is to apply decorative panelling to one or more of the walls.

Using a tape measure and level, divide the wall into equal panels **[a]**, marking each one off clearly on the wall with a pencil **[b]**. Stand back and make sure that the panel spacing is equal before you proceed any further.

To make an absolutely perfect job of the panelling, draw the wall and panels to scale on a piece of graph paper before you start. This will create the right balance between the positions of the panels before you transfer the dimensions onto the walls.

A mitre saw provides a quick and effective way of cutting the various sections of softwood dado rail needed to make the panelling **[c]**. Alternatively, use a mitre box and tenon saw to create the same sections.

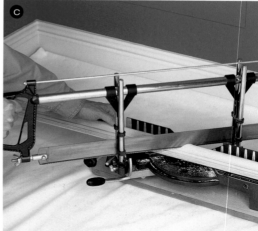

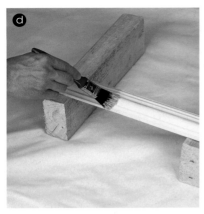

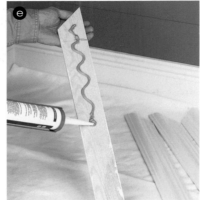

After sandpapering the cut wood to the desired smoothness, apply knotting fluid with a brush to any knots in the wood. This process effectively prevents the knots from shrinking and falling out when the heating is turned on and the wood dries out. Paint bare wood with a wood primer **[d]** before applying undercoat and topcoats of the desired colour. Make sure that you allow the paint to dry completely between coats.

As a rule, it is a good idea always to use two coats of undercoat before applying the topcoat finish. Use very fine sandpaper, known as flour paper, in between coats, to remove any dust and debris and create the perfect finish.

To fix the timber sections to the wall simply and effectively, apply 'Liquid Nails' or 'No Nails'

MUST KNOW

Tools required
Tape measure
Spirit level
Mitre saw or
    mitre block and
    tenon saw
Adhesive
Wood glue
Sponge
Sandpaper
Paint brush

WATCH OUT!

Excessive adhesive
One of the mistakes commonly made by DIY-ers who are new to basic joinery is to use too much adhesive when fixing lengths of wood. If adhesive is allowed to squeeze out from beneath the panelling and onto the walls, it can be a nightmare to clean up and subsequently very unsightly.

PAINTING & DECORATING

43

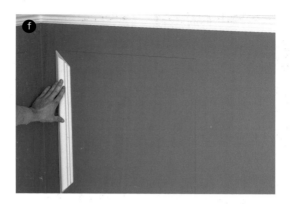

44

adhesive to the back of the cut lengths **[e]** and squeeze them carefully into place on the wall **[f]**. These are the proprietary names of the two most suitable adhesives for this kind of job, although there are others available. Join the lengths to each other to complete the panel by using PVA whitewood glue on the cut mitre ends.

If you have taken your time and done the job with care, the mitres you have cut should fit together perfectly. However, if this is not the case, use some wood filler to make good any gaps, applying it to the mitres with the tip of your finger **[g]**. Wipe off any excess filler with a damp sponge. Alternatively, you could squeeze some decorator's caulk into the mitre joints,

---

MUST KNOW

A good match?
Think carefully about the style of panelling you select before actually purchasing it. Choose panelling that will tie in well with your existing skirting boards, as well as any picture or dado rails that might already be on the walls. The same applies to extant cornices and coving.

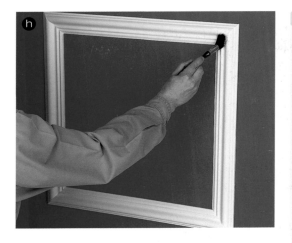

MUST KNOW

Style guides

If you wish to emulate a particular historical period with the panelling you apply, ask your supplier to explain the different styles of architrave available and check out design websites and home style magazines for advice on what is most fashionable at the time.

again wiping off the excess with a damp sponge. This method can be most effective.

Repeat the process described on all the walls to which you want to add panelling. Allow the adhesive to dry fully and then give it a light rub down with the flour paper. Apply a final finish coat of paint **[h]**.

To make the most of your panelling, why not try some alternative decor so that it stands out from the surrounding wall? Within the panel, the world's your oyster. To contrast with the principal wall colour, you could choose a simple painted colour change, perhaps a piece of patterned wallpaper, a series of landscapes across several panels or perhaps a stylish *trompe l'oeil* effect as a real talking point.

Tongue and groove panelling is good for covering a badly plastered wall or old tiles that are difficult to remove. There are some stylish and unusual designs available on the market today. One perennial favourite is the bead and butt design, which is archetypally Victorian. For an inexpensive alternative, try complete sections of panelling which are simply made up of MDF sheets and then routed out to imitate the real thing. These are relatively cheap, but can look good.

want to know more?

Take it to the next level...

Go to...

▶ **Repairing windows** – pages 102–3
▶ **Replacing skirting** – pages 80–1
▶ **Repairing a gate** – pages 156–7

Other sources

▶ **DIY advice**
   check out the 'How to' library in B&Q's online website: www.diy.com
▶ **Products on the Internet**
   visit www.decoratingdirect.co.uk for decorating materials delivered direct to your door
▶ **DIY courses**
   look into a City & Guilds qualification in Painting & Decorating

fixtures &

fittings

DIY is synonymous with home improvements, some of the easiest of which can be effected by the installation of new fixtures and fittings or the adaptation of existing features. In this chapter, we show you how to put things up or get them into better shape!

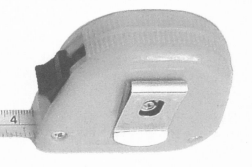

Hanging pictures & making a simple frame

One of the simplest of all DIY tasks is hanging pictures, but to make the job more challenging and rewarding, why not make your own picture frame before hanging it up?

Making a picture frame

To give a print or picture a bit of something extra, use a mounting card, maybe in a contrasting colour. This method is particularly useful if you wish to make the picture itself become the focal point. The eye is naturally drawn in to the artwork. Cut the mounting card to the overall size you want, and mark out the section that you wish to remove to allow as much of the picture to be revealed as you want. This cut-out is achieved by using a bevel-mount cutter, or alternatively a flat metal square and a craft knife **[a]**. You can also purchase ready-cut mounts from any picture supplier.

Using a mitre saw (or a tenon saw and mitre box) cut the picture frame section to suit your card size, allowing for external mitres at the end of each piece in your calculations **[b]**. Glue and pin the four sections together; there are special corner-angled staples available to connect the sections together **[c]**. Position the glass, mounting card with picture taped in place, and

MUST KNOW
Tools required
Tape measure
Flat steel square
Hammer
Mitre saw (tenon saw and mitre block)
Hammer drill
Masonry bits
Craft knife
Bradawl
Wire cutters or pliers

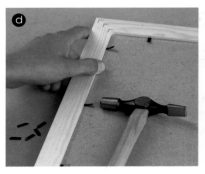

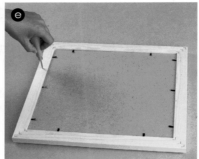

the backing (which can be cut from hardboard), then tap in the spring frame clips **[d]**.

Use a bradawl to make the holes in the back of the frame for screwing in the eyelets **[e]** and connect the string or picture wire to the eyelets to mount your artwork on a picture hook.

If you are attempting to hang an extremely heavy piece of artwork, or maybe a tapestry wall hanging, the fixing will have to be substantial. Carefully decide on the hanging position. Using a hammer drill and masonry bit **[f]** (the masonry bit must match the rawl plug size), use either a conventional screw with a minimum length of 50mm (2in) with about 25 per cent of its total length protruding to hang the artwork upon, or a heavy duty hook screwed into the rawl plug to ensure that your picture remains securely in place.

For average-weight pictures and prints, conventional picture hooks with masonry pins are available from any DIY store or picture-framing suppliers, and these are fixed by tapping them gently into the wall with a hammer **[g]**.

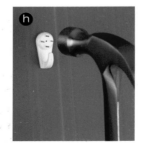

Modern plastic hooks with four smaller pins for fixing are available as an alternative to hooks and pins. These can be bought from any hardware or DIY store and are fixed in the same way as conventional hooks **[h]**.

Fitting curtain rails & poles

After decorating, it is often a good idea to renew dirty old curtain rails and poles. Alternatively, you may just want to replace your existing rails with something more decorative.

Fixing a pole

A wooden pole will come with two ring type brackets, which the pole is suspended between. The rings will fit into round wall fixings, which will have holes through the middle to fix them to the wall. Firstly, establish a point above the head of the window where you would like your curtains to hang from, say 100mm (4in). Mark the line with a straight piece of wood and spirit level. Now mark a point at the centre of the window. Having established your line, you should decide where you want your fixings along the pole. Measure the pole then divide the distance by four. Measure the distance one side of the centre and mark. Repeat for the other side and you have your fixing points.

Remember, your screws should be long enough to fix right into the masonry as well as the plaster, plus the depth of the fixing hole in the ring fixing. Drill your holes and insert plugs.

MUST KNOW
Tools required
Drill
Masonry bit
Plugs and screws
Steel self-tapping
screws
Spirit level

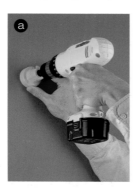

Fix the round wall fixings to the wall **[a]**.

Next, fit the wood support ring to the wall fixing, using screws to secure one to the other **[b]**. Remember to thread the pole through the rings first and don't forget also to thread

the curtain rings onto the pole, spacing these at a suitable distance along the length of the pole. Lastly, you can fit the end stops to the pole, securing with the small screws supplied with the pole **[c]**.

Fixing a curtain track

When you buy a curtain rail, it will usually come with a sufficient number of fixing brackets to support its length. So the number of brackets supplied will normally establish the spacing along the track. Measure the length of the track and if necessary cut it to suit the window first. As for the pole, the same applies to the track. Mark a level line at a suitable point above the window head to hang your curtains.

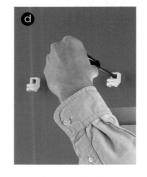

Screw each bracket along your line **[d]**. The track will snap over the brackets, starting at the top and working from one end **[e]**. Having fixed the rail, you can now slip the gliders along the track. Push and screw the end stop gliders into place **[f]**. Hang your curtains from the gliders.

Fitting a fireplace surround

A fireplace surround can either be used to enhance an existing feature or as a decorative 'dummy' feature on a bare wall. A fireplace is not strictly required.

You do not need to attach a fireplace surround to a chimney breast – the surround can fit straight onto a wall. However, this must be an external wall if you intend to fit a gas fire within the surround. If you really want a chimney breast to go with the fireplace surround, you could build a dummy breast for effect, and fit the fire surround to that. However, if you are lucky enough to have a chimney breast in the room, then that is the place to fix the fire surround.

The surround featured in the photographs on these pages is purely decorative and can be fixed to a straight wall or chimney breast. This surround is purchased as a kit, with a pine surround and imitation marble insert and hearth.

Begin by putting a centre mark on both the wall and the hearth so that they align **[a]**. Turn the hearth on to its face, first ensuring that the face is protected with a dustsheet, then apply adhesive or silicone mastic to the hearth framework **[b]** and fix it into position, using the alignment marks **[c]**. Next, check it is level.

Place the mantel assembly upside down; slide the legs into position, and then screw the block inside the mantel assembly **[d]**. To secure the legs, first check they are square to the mantel and then screw them in place with 6 x 35mm (1⅜in) screws.

For a simple method of fixing this surround to the wall, screw two mirror plates with screws to

the back edge of the legs, approximately 230mm (9in) from the top **[e]**. Next fix the marble effect insert to the surround as shown, with screws approximately 380mm (15in) apart **[f]**. Remember to pre-drill pilot holes for the screws to avoid break-out damage.

Hold the surround up to the wall and mark the hole positions through the mirror plates **[g]**. Remove the surround, drill and plug the wall, and then fix the surround with screws.

To complete the job, place the reveal insert into position, to cover the wall behind and leave a clean, neat finish to the surround as a whole **[h]**.

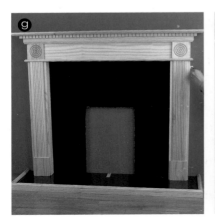

FIXTURES & FITTINGS

53

Putting up shelves

This is one of those DIY jobs that people always think is very easy. However, there is more to shelf installation than meets the eye, and badly put up shelves are always very unsightly.

Try to work out roughly what sort of weight you may be loading onto the shelves you intend to put up and construct them accordingly.

The spur shelving system shown on this page is a pre-finished adjustable shelf system, made from mild steel, consisting of vertical wall mounted sections with angled support sections, which simply hook into the wall mounted uprights to create a strong and efficient shelving system.

To fix the spur type of shelving, you first need to fix the vertical supports level and parallel. To achieve this, fix at the top, without tightening the screw right home, plumb it straight with a spirit level, mark and fix the bottom screw. Check that the upright is level when it is against the wall and use packing pieces behind the supports for adjustment if necessary. Tightly screw home all the fixing points on the upright.

Using the spirit level, match the top of the second upright to the first **[a]** and repeat the fixing process **[b]**.

Next, hook in the shelf supports at the desired heights, then simply cut the shelves to length and attach them to the support brackets via the fixing positions on the undersides of the brackets **[c]**.

The other system of shelving shown here is simply a made-up shelf system which is fixed to the wall, with the fixing positions concealed from the eye. This is known simply as a 'ladder frame' system.

Fixed shelving can be easily installed by using the ladder frame system. Mark the shelf positions with a spirit level on all three sides of the alcove, cut a batten to length and fix it in place on the wall with screws and plugs **[d]**. Next, fix the two side battens, using the same method **[e]**. Cut the fourth batten to length and fix with two screws at each end into the side battens **[f]**. Cut and fix the central support. The rear screws will have to be fixed at an angle **[g]**, the front screws fixed in the normal way. To add extra strength, use PVA glue at the fixing points. The shelf width may determine how many central cross supports you need, and this is the reason for the term 'ladder frame'. Put simply, the wider the shelf, the more central cross supports are required, so that the structure resembles a ladder.

Cut the shelf board to size, measuring from the front of the shelf to the wall, then fix it in place with PVA glue and pins – or from underneath with screws to conceal the fixing positions. Use a couple of fast cramps to hold the board in position during fixing.

Finally, to dress the front edge, use a section of wooden moulding, glued and pinned or screwed from underneath the shelf for concealed fixing **[h]**.

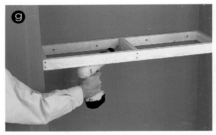

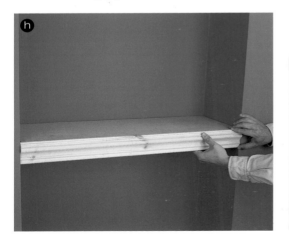

MUST KNOW

Tools required
Spirit level
Drill
Masonry bit
Hammer
Screwdriver
Saw
Tape measure
Sandpaper

Assembling flatpacks

When it comes to assembly, flatpacks come in varying degrees of difficulty. However, basic principles apply to most and they should not be beyond the skills of the average DIY-er.

Ideally, flatpacks are best assembled on a workbench – provided that the components of the pack are not too large to work with in this way. If the latter is the case, or you do not have a workbench, create a large clear space on a hard floor, as shown here. Read the instructions carefully and gather together all the tools that you will need prior to embarking on the assembly of the flatpack.

On these pages we show two common flat pack assemblies – a wooden upright storage system (a shelf unit) and a kitchen base unit. A shelf system is very easy to assemble and a good way of making a start in DIY. Attach two of the uprights to the top and bottom shelves with the screws supplied, through the pre-drilled pilot holes **[a]**. Turn the shelving system over and attach the remaining two uprights as above **[b]**. Next, simply insert the remaining shelves to the desired height and screw through the pre-drilled

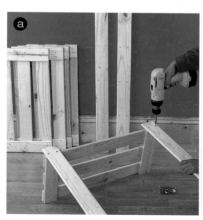
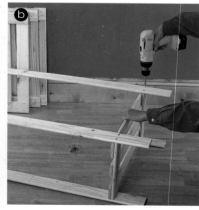

positions. Turn the shelving system over and
screw the shelves tight.

Stand the shelf system upright and secure it
to the wall to prevent the unit from falling over if
it is knocked **[c]**.

Nearly all kitchen flatpacks are variations on a
basic theme. You will normally need the same
set of tools and skills to assemble any individual
unit that you purchase. Here, we demonstrate
how to put together a standard 500mm (19¾in)
base unit. Open up and assemble one unit at a

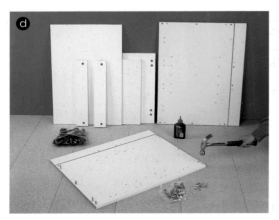

FIXTURES & FITTINGS

57

WATCH OUT!

Collateral damage

Many flatpacks are made from relatively cheap materials and can be damaged very easily. White vinyl or laminated surfaces often conceal interiors of cheap chipboard, which will crumble easily if screwed too tight or will split with the pressure of a badly aligned screw. Be careful as you put them together!

time, then fit them all together to make up your kitchen. Next, fit the worktops and, finally, hang the doors.

Lay the side panel face down onto the bench or floor. Apply PVA glue to the dowels and tap them home **[d]** (see page 57, bottom). Also screw in the special connecting bolts, top and bottom where indicated. Repeat this process for the second panel.

In this case, the bottom panel and top connecting rails have pre-drilled fixing positions for the connecting bolt locking nuts. There is an indicator arrow on the locking nut. Ensure that the arrow points to the outer edge **[e]**. Apply glue to the dowels, place the end panels and connecting rails into position and tighten the

bolts securely [f].
Connect the second
side panel by using
the same method.

To fix the back
panel to the unit, first
run a small bead of
glue the length of both
slots and slide the
back panel into
position. Carefully drill
two pilot holes into the
top rail and secure
with two 15mm (⅝in)
screws. Wipe off any
excess glue with a
damp cloth.

Turn the cabinet
upside down and fix
the adjustable legs, by

screwing the four
plastic lugs with three
screws in each lug.
Finally, screw in the
adjustable legs [g].
Turn the cabinet onto
its legs, ensuring that
they have been
secured tightly and
that the unit will be
stable when it is set in
place. Check for
plumbness with a spirit
level. Insert shelf
supports at the
required height – there
is normally a choice of
heights – then tilt and
slide in the shelf [h].

Adapting a cupboard for more storage space

One of the great advantages of being able to do jobs for yourself is that you can improve existing features and save a fortune into the bargain. Making the most of an understairs cupboard is a rewarding job to undertake and a home improvement that offers invaluable extra storage space.

Decide what you need to store in the cupboard, measure out the space **[a]** and draw it onto a piece of paper, carefully dividing the space into sections for efficient storage.

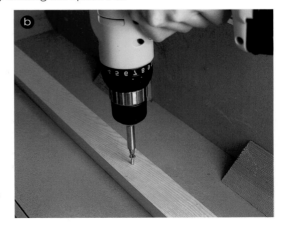

Fix a softwood batten to the underside of the stairs and a second one to the floor to fix the partition panel onto **[b]**. Pre-drill the panels and countersink the screws. Add a bead of PVA glue for extra

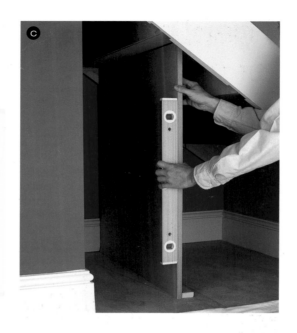

MUST KNOW

Tools required
Measuring tape
Saw
Square
Spirit level
Drill
Masonry and wood
 drill bits
Hammer
Screwdriver

strength. Ensure that the partition is level using either a spirit level **[c]**, or a plumb line.

To create one or more shelves in the space, fit the required number of battens to both sides, using a level to ensure that they match. The shelves and panels that you use can be made of MDF or any other timber sheet material – a minimum of 18mm (¾in)

thick **[d]**. Additional strength can be added to the shelf by fitting a batten underneath the front edge of the shelf and a batten fitted to the back wall of the cupboard.

Using 50 x 50mm (2 x 2in) PAR, cut and fit two side rails to the cupboard; take care

FIXTURES & FITTINGS

61

to scribe over the skirting, if the skirting is to remain. Fix the rails with plugs and screws.

Use 50 x 25mm (2 x 1in) PAR for the remaining top and bottom rails of the frame, and screw these to the underside of the stairs and the floor **[e]**.

To form the cupboard door, cut a piece of MDF, plywood or block board to the shape of the opening. Do not fit the door too snugly, as board will frequently expand and contract in centrally heated houses, which could cause the door to stick if it has been fitted too tightly. Simple flush hinges can be used to hang the door **[f]**, as it is a cupboard door which will be subject to only infrequent use.

To complete the job, fit a doorknob and a pair of magnetic catches to the

Sensible shapes and sizes

Think about what you want to store in your understairs cupboard before adapting it. These spaces tend to be unusual in shape, and there is no point in dividing the area up into lots of odd-shaped little compartments if you then discover that your vacuum cleaner, or whatever, will no longer fit.

Best board

Use the best board that you can afford for the cupboard door. It will look better, give a superior finish and will be less prone to warping.

cupboard door **[g]**. If you want a more ornate finish to the cupboard door, add a pine moulding to form panels before you begin painting it. The panel moulding shape should be drawn onto the door first. Cut to suit the drawn shape, using a jigsaw for any shapes involving curves, and then glue the moulding onto the door using a powerful adhesive.

Allow everything to dry thoroughly before painting the door to finish the job.

FIXTURES & FITTINGS

63

Installing sliding wardrobe doors

Sliding wardrobe doors are a worthwhile space-saving feature which also maximise storage space in wardrobes. They can look good and enhance a bedroom, too, if made from good quality materials and equipped with mirrors. Perhaps surprisingly, a basic system is not difficult to install.

A range of sliding wardrobe door systems are available as ready-made packages, as are independent track systems for various standard doors, or even for creating a custom-made design of your own. Here we show you how to fit a very simple door and track package that will work very well in any standard wardrobe.

Using a tape measure and pencil [a], mark the dimensions of the wardrobe on the walls and ceiling with the aid of a spirit level. The minimum internal depth of the wardrobe should be 600mm (24in) and the floor to ceiling height should be 2286mm (90in). If your ceiling height is more than 2286mm (90in), it will be necessary to build an infill down from the ceiling to obtain the 2286mm (90in) overall

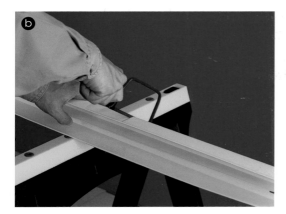

height. Do not attempt to raise the bottom track above floor level.

Cut the ceiling and floor tracks to the required opening width to ensure flush alignment with the end walls **[b]**. Skirting boards can be cut to allow the doors to close against the wall, or alternatively fit a batten to the wall. Fix the ceiling track securely, preferably through the ceiling into the ceiling joists, but if this is not practicable, use proper plasterboard fixings **[c]**. When fixing the ceiling track, remember to allow for 10mm (⅜in) fascia thickness in your calculations. Using the screwdriver, fix the top guides to the

doors with the screws provided, as shown on the end rails **[d]** (see bottom right, page 65).

Position the rear sliding door first, by placing the top of the door into the rear guide of the top track. This is achieved by angling the door into the top track with the bottom of the door held away from the bottom track **[e]**. When the top

FIXTURES & FITTINGS

guides are in position, place the bottom of the door onto the bottom track rear guide. Use a spirit level against the door to ensure the accurate positioning of the bottom track **[f]**. With the bottom track perfectly in line, simply fix with the screws provided **[g]**, ensuring that the track does not slip out of line as you fix it to the bedroom floor. Check that the doors run smoothly and make any corrections as necessary.

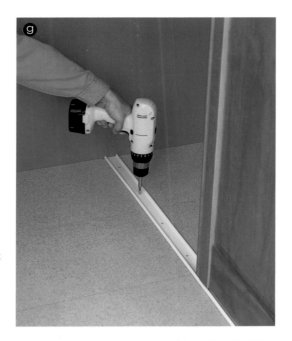

Cut the timber fascia to the required length. Clean the front face of the ceiling track with a solvent (white spirit) and allow it to dry. Pre-packaged fascias normally come with adhesive strips as standard. Carefully remove the backing paper from the fascia adhesive tape, and then press the fascia board onto the ceiling track face, applying pressure along the length for good adhesion **[h]**.

Installing a loft ladder

If you use your loft for storage space, then a permanent loft ladder is a good idea. Even if this is not the case, a ladder will prove useful if you ever need to access your cold water storage tank, which will normally be found in the loft.

Loft ladders are generally made to suit three different ceiling heights – 2.3m (7ft 7in), 2.5m (8ft 3in) and 2.9–3m (9ft 6in–10ft). They normally operate on a slide and fold basis, or are the concertina type, which tend to be a little more complicated and prone to sticking. Some loft ladders even incorporate a handrail. The type illustrated on these pages is a slide ladder, with a handrail fitted as standard. It may not be

WATCH OUT!

Enough space?
Before you purchase your loft ladder, it is important to measure a series of dimensions both in the hatch and the loft itself to ensure that the ladder you select will fit properly. Lofts come in all shapes and sizes, so there is no such thing as a standard fit. Make sure you have sufficient clearance space in the loft and a big enough hatch.

exactly the same make as your own chosen ladder but the principle is the same, and in any case, each ladder should come with its own fitting instructions.

The loft trapdoor must be hinged to open downwards, so the hinges provided must be fixed to the same side of the opening as the loft ladder **[a]**. The trapdoor should be made from 19mm (¾in) plywood, MDF or blockboard and must

be fitted flush with the ceiling.

Lower the ladder to the floor. Engage the catches and make sure they are locked in position. Fit the loft ladder guide assembly to the frame with the screws provided **[b]** and **[c]**. Make sure that the climbing angle is correct by checking the special angle indicator on the side of the ladder. Slide down the two plastic stops to the top of the guide assembly and

tighten all four screws **[d]**. This will ensure that the ladder is always in the correct position for climbing into the loft.

Fix the pivot arm to the floor of the loft **[e]**. Close the three sections together, making sure the catches lock in position, and push the ladder up fully into the loft. Slide the two plastic stops up to the underside of the guide assembly and tighten the four screws **[f]**. This ensures that the ladder clears the trapdoor when it is closed. Attach the handrails to either side of the middle or top section **[g]**.

WATCH OUT!

Adjust as required
Be careful when first pulling the ladder down – it might land on top of you! Adjust the sliding action as necessary.

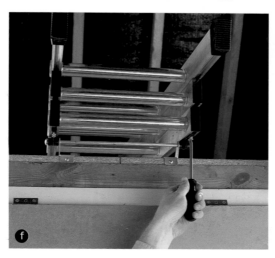

To fix the automatic latch for the trapdoor, position the latch in the centre of the frame surround and opposite the trapdoor hinges [h]. The latch must be set back by the thickness of the trapdoor.

Engage the pointed marker into the latch and close the trap door. The correct position for fixing the striking plate is where the point marks the trap door. Test the position by opening and closing the trapdoor until you are completely happy with the action [i].

FIXTURES & FITTINGS

Fixing a laminate floor

Wooden laminate floors have become very popular in recent years and can now be purchased inexpensively in kit form from a wide range of DIY stores and other outlets. They come in many styles and are surprisingly easy to fit.

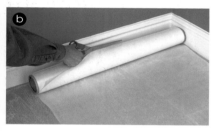

Firstly, repair any damage to the existing floor and screw down any loose boards. Check for pipes before fixing down any loose boards. Use a pilot drill and countersink bit to guide the screws.

Ideally, the best way to start is to remove the skirting before you begin laying the new floor. You can lay the floor with the skirting in place, as shown, provided an 8mm (⅜in) clearance from the skirting is left all around the floor edge.

New laminate flooring is supplied with a separate foam base on a roll, approximately 6mm (¼in) thick **[a]**, which you simply cut to size and lay on top of the existing floor **[b]**.

Lay the first board against the wall leaving an 8mm (⅜in) gap between the board and the wall by using pre-cut wooden spacers **[c]**. Cutting a section to length, simply measure (remember the 8mm gap), mark with a square and cut with either a tenon saw or crosscut saw **[d]**. Ensure that the saw is sharp. To avoid breakout, score the surface with a craft knife on the line before cutting with the saw. You can use offcuts to fill awkward corners of the floor, so wastage of materials should be kept to a minimum. Obviously, very short offcuts may not be worth using.

Apply the glue to the end tongue only and complete the first line. Then apply the second line of boards by applying the adhesive along the length as well as the end of the tongue **[e]**. The flooring is made with a tongue and groove design, which interlocks together for strength, with minimum waste.

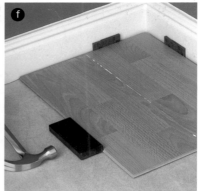

Once positioned onto the glued tongue, the board should be tapped home using a claw hammer and a tapping block to tighten up the joints **[f]**. Wipe away any excess glue **[g]**.

Continue this process across the room until you have finished the floor. You may have to cut the last board along its length to fit the room (remember to allow for the wooden spacers). When the floor is finished, leave for a minimum of 6 hours to allow the adhesive to cure properly. Then remove the wooden spacers all around. This is very important to allow the floor to expand and contract unrestricted. Finally, cut 20mm (¾in) quadrant to size; apply a thin bead of glue to the skirting face of the quadrant and pin to the skirting ONLY to cover the gap all around, but still allowing the floor to move **[h]**.

MUST KNOW

Tools required
Scissors
Tape measure
Pencil
Hand saw
Set square
Craft knife
Claw hammer
Tapping block
Spacers

Fixing vinyl floor tiles

Vinyl floor tiles offer an inexpensive alternative to ceramic, stone or wooden floorcoverings and come in an array of attractive designs. These tiles are not particularly difficult to lay, but great care is needed in order to achieve a good result.

Vinyl tiles are much easier to use than their linoleum predecessors and similar materials. In the case of a conventional boarded wooden floor, it is necessary to overlay the floor first either with hardboard or 6mm (¼in) plywood. Plywood is the best option. It is not much more expensive than hardboard, but makes a better job. Fix the plywood or hardboard with 25mm (1in) ring nails.

Vinyl tiles are normally self-adhesive, but store the tiles in the room for a couple of days for them to acclimatize to the room temperature. Mark the centre of two opposite walls and snap a chalk line or string between the two points **[a]**. Repeat this on the opposite two walls and there you have your centre point. Lay out some tiles at this point, without removing the protective backing, to see the most effective way of fixing them with minimum wastage and balanced cut edges.

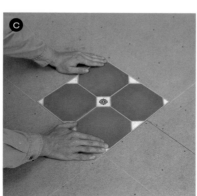

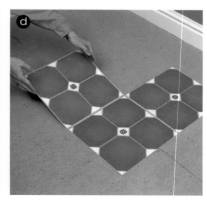

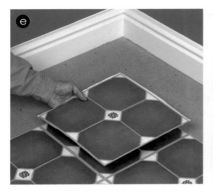

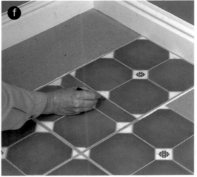

Mark your starting position. Lift the tiles and give the floor a final vacuum. Peel the backing off the first tile **[b]** and carefully place to the marks applying smoothing pressure with your hands **[c]**. Repeat the process, concentrating on one half of the floor and steadily laying a pyramid shape, carefully butting the tiles together **[d]**.

For trimming in the edges, lay a tile against the wall over the last full tile **[e]** (without removing the backing) and mark the fixed tile **[f]**. Transfer the marks onto a tile for cutting with a sharp craft knife and a straight edge **[g]**. Peel the backing paper off and stick the cut tile firmly into place **[h]**. Finally, tidy up any rough or straggly tile edges with the craft knife and straight edge.

MUST KNOW

Tools required
Hammer
Chalk line
Straight edge
Craft knife
Measuring tape

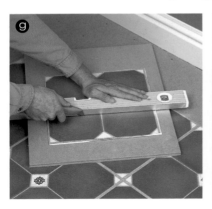

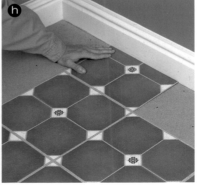

Fixing ceramic floor tiles

Ceramic floor tiles can be expensive, but they will bring a touch of class to your room. One consideration to bear in mind is that they can be cold underfoot. However, it is possible to fit basic underfloor heating prior to laying the tiles.

Mark the centre of all four walls and snap a chalk line on the floor to dissect the floor to be tiled into quarters. Lay the tiles out dry in one quarter, then mark the floor for fixing two wooden battens. It is very important that the battens are perfectly square. Check this by using the 3:4:5 method. Mark off one batten at 3ft (915mm) and the second batten at 4ft (1220mm); measuring between the two points should equal exactly 5ft (1520mm). The corner should be perfectly square, so secure the battens and apply the adhesive about a square yard (metre) at a time with a serrated trowel **[a]**. Press the tiles into the adhesive, building out from the corner. Use spacers between the tiles to form equal size joints **[b]**. Use a short straight edge (spirit level) to check the tiles are in line **[c]**. Repeat this process until the whole floor area is covered. Leave for 24 hours to

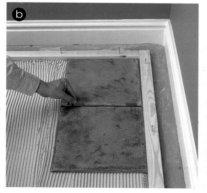

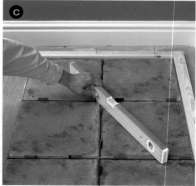

cure, then carefully remove the battens to cut in the edges all round.

Carefully measure both ends of the tile space, and transfer the dimensions to a tile for cutting **[d]**. Remember to allow for spacers and cut with a mechanical tile cutter **[e]**. Paste the back of the tile with adhesive and squeeze carefully into place. Check the edge tiles are level with the rest of the tiled floor.

Grout the new tiled floor with a waterproof grout using a rubber float, wiping off the excess with a damp sponge, and rinsing regularly **[f]**. Compress and shape the joints as necessary. When the grout has cured, give it a final clean and polish with a soft cloth.

Finally, apply a silicone mastic joint between the floor and the walls all around the room, as a seal.

MUST KNOW

Tools required
Screwdriver
Measuring tape
Hammer
Pencil
Serrated edge trowel
Rubber float
Sponge
Tile cutter
Straight edge

want to know **more?**

Take it to the next level...

Go to...
▶ **Fitting wall lights** – pages 142–5
▶ **Sanding floors** – pages 82–7
▶ **Cupboard doors** – pages 90–3

Other sources
▶ **Picture framing classes**
   look for courses in your local paper
▶ **Magazines**
   have a look at as many different house style magazines as possible to get ideas for your own home
▶ **Manufacturer's booklets**
   product leaflets can offer inspiration
▶ **Internet**
   visit www.thehouseplanner.co.uk

general

repairs

DIY is not just about embarking on new projects and creating things from scratch – it also involves maintaining and repairing existing features to keep them in the best possible condition. In this chapter, we show you how.

Replacing & repairing skirting

Skirting boards are essential for making walls look complete. They cover the joint between the wall and the floor and double as a decorative feature. There will be times when you need to repair them or wish to replace them.

Repairing damaged skirting

Sometimes it is possible to cut out a piece of skirting and replace it 'in situ', without having to take everything apart. To do this, firstly knock the blade of a small bolster chisel behind the skirting. Lever open a gap to allow the crowbar to fit and place a wooden packer behind the crowbar to protect the wall from damage when levering. Slide a couple of timber blocks down behind the skirting to keep the skirting sprung from the wall **[a]**. Position the mitre block against the skirting and, using the 45° slot, cut the skirting with a tenon saw, using short strokes **[b]**. Repeat this process to the other side of the damage and remove the damaged piece of skirting.

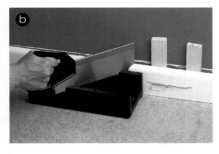

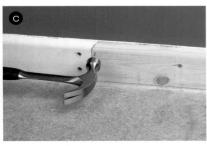

Release the blocks and countersink and screw the skirting back into position into wall plugs. Carefully measure the distance, or use the damaged piece of skirting as a template (remember to allow extra for the saw cuts if you do). Begin driving in the pins and add a bead of PVA glue. Hold in position and knock home the pins **[c]**. Use a pin punch to drive in the pins and a damp cloth to wipe off any excess glue. Use a filler on the pin holes and joints and allow to dry. Sandpaper down, prime, undercoat and top-coat for a successful repair. This method is what is know in the building trade as 'scarfing'.

Replacing skirting

Removing the entire skirting involves simply repeating the process mentioned above, moving the levers along and springing the skirting free from the middle **[d]**. Once the first piece is freed, the rest should spring free fairly easily in sequence.

To make a good job of replacing skirting, you will need a mitre saw, which will come in handy for other jobs as well. If you are very fortunate and the internal corners of your walls are perfectly square, it may be possible to cut a really tight and professional-looking internal mitre **[e]**. However, it does take time to master a mitre saw. It is sometimes possible to fix skirting directly into masonry or brickwork with masonry nails, but you may find battens easier **[f]**.

An external mitre should be cut, glued and pinned together, ensuring a perfect square fit and closed joint **[g]**. For extra strength, fix a couple of pins through the mitre itself **[h]**.

MUST KNOW

Tools required

Small bolster chisel
Crowbar
Tenon saw
Mitre block
Coping saw
Pencil
Tape measure
Drill
Countersink
Square
Claw hammer
Pinchers
Nail and pin punch
Mitre saw

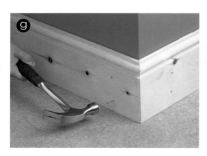

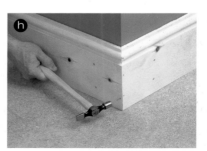

Replacing/repairing damaged floorboards

You may be daunted by the prospect of tearing up and replacing your floorboards, but the job is actually not nearly as difficult as it might seem. Sometimes it is possible to repair sections of board without lifting the entire floor.

Firstly, and probably most importantly, if you are choosing to expose your groundfloor boards, do remember that almost all wooden (board type) floors are suspended floors. This means that the floorboards are fixed (generally nailed) to a supporting framework of timber joists, which are in turn supported and suspended from the ground by small brick walls. Very importantly, these floors have air vents to the front and rear of the property to allow unhindered air circulation, which prevents infestation by woodworm, wet and dry rot, and other common problems.

Over a period of time as the sap in the floorboards dries out, the boards tend to shrink and gaps form in between them. In the winter this can cause uncomfortable draughts and you might also find regular and unsightly deposits of dust on your furniture as well. Floors on the upper levels of houses are not normally affected in this way because they are closed-in floors and no ventilation is necessary.

If your property has had central heating fitted, or been rewired, or both, when you take up the carpets you might well find that the floorboards are in a very untidy state. Most plumbers and electricians are motivated by speed to finish the job, so they tend to pay little respect to floorboards, particularly if they would appear to be hidden by other floor coverings. They rip up

GENERAL REPAIRS

MUST KNOW

Tools required
Cordless drill
2 flat-type nail bars
Claw hammer
Pinchers
Cramps
Wood chisel
Tenon saw
Hand saw
Electric sander
PVA wood glue
Pins
Floor brads

the boards cutting the wood where convenient, to suit their own purposes (often cutting two boards on the same joint), and breaking pieces off when lifting the boards.

Although this is really not a major problem under carpets, it certainly will be once the boards are exposed as a decorative feature.

WATCH OUT!

Broken nails
Old floorboards in particular are often a graveyard of old, bent and sometimes rusty nails. These can be a nuisance or even dangerous...

Removing damaged floorboards

Carefully remove the skirtings that are fitted around the area of floorboards to be replaced or repaired. (Refer to Replacing Skirtings, pages 80–1.) This will allow easier lifting of the boards.

Removing the first board is the most difficult. Carefully insert the nail bars on opposite sides of the board and central to the length (if necessary tap with a claw hammer) and lever the board upwards **[a]**. Use wooden blocks for extra leverage – this will also help to prevent damage to the adjacent boards **[b]**.

Repeat this process along the length of the wooden floor. Starting at the middle will help spring each board away from the joists. Once the first board is removed, access is easier for the removal of all the others, using exactly the same technique.

Repairing and replacing boards

You can cut out any damaged sections in a square form to simplify a replacement. Carefully mark the board around the damaged section using a square **[c]**. Use two wooden battens to keep the rogue board supported above the floor, allowing the damaged section to be cut out using a tenon saw **[d]**.

Mark and cut a matching piece from another board. Cut the replacement section 2mm (⅛in) oversize, to ensure a tight fit with no gaps. Use a wooden block and hammer to tap the replacement section into position. Nail the new board in place **[e]**. Smooth with a sander or by hand using sandpaper and a block.

To replace wooden floorboards, remove all the old nails from the joists using the nail bars and a claw hammer **[f]**. Clumsy use of the claw hammer will result in damage to the joists – even with the protection of the nail bars – so take care as you lever out the old nails. Drill fine pilot holes in your new boards to prevent splitting in the wood and to locate and direct the position of the fixings **[g]**. Stagger the cut boards to avoid two joints abutting side by side – this not only bonds the floor better and assists the support of the boards, but looks better, as well. Secure with floor brad nails **[h]**.

Sanding floors

In order to get the best from your bare floorboards, it may well be necessary to sand away old varnish, woodstain and other floor treatments. You will need a sander for this job.

Wooden flooring has steadily increased in popularity – both solid and laminate-type floors. Normal laminate floors cannot be sanded down, because the surface is only a few millimetres thick of formica, and below that is the sub-strata of MDF or chipboard. Sanding and lacquering the old original floorboards is particularly popular. It's noisy, dusty, messy and hard work, but it can be very rewarding.

The first job is to inspect the condition of the floorboards. Tap down the floorboard fixing nails with a suitable nail punch **[a]** and remove any other nails or screws. All this will help to avoid tearing the sanding belts.

If woodworm has attacked the floor, lift the boards carefully, treat the joists and the back and front of the contaminated boards, and then re-fix. Sanding and lacquering over the woodworm gives the floor 'character'. If the woodworm is too severe or a board is damaged, cut it down in length or patch in a

GENERAL REPAIRS

86

repair using wood glue and pins or a clamp. Any repairs or replacements should be done using the same floorboards. Replacements can be taken from elsewhere in the house or from a reclamation yard. New boards simply will not match and will leave your floor looking like a patchwork quilt.

Lay the floor drum sander on its back (unplugged); undo the retaining bar and fix the sanding belt **[b]**; screw it down tightly to avoid the belt working loose. There are three grades of sandpaper to choose from – coarse, medium and fine. Unless the boards are very rough, you may only need to use medium and fine grades.

If the boards have 'cupped' (curled), this can be tackled by running the belt sander across the room at a 45° angle **[c]** and again at 45° from the other angle. When the floor is perfectly flat, use a fine belt and sand along the board length and grain **[d]**.

Hire an edging sander to sand the edges where the drum sander is unable to reach. The pads are fitted to the machine by a central bolt on the underside **[e]**. Avoid overrunning this machine on the floor **[f]**, as if so you may leave swirl scratches on the face of the floorboards. Use the hook scraper for awkward, tight areas of the floor or in corners **[g]**.

Re-aligning kitchen cupboard doors

Over a period of time and with repeated use, kitchen doors will drop on their hinges and become misaligned. Most hinges have a built-in adjustment feature which is easy to correct.

Making adjustments to the doors of your kitchen units is an easy and simple operation. Most standard mass-produced kitchens are supplied with plumb hinges. These are hinges that are cut into the back face of the door, spring-loaded to fit over a hinge plate that's attached to the cabinet itself. Constant opening and closing over a period of time can cause the doors to drop out of alignment, hence the need to make adjustments.

There are three areas of door adjustment on a cabinet hinge. The first is the large central screw that you use to attach the door to the cabinet. This screw tightens down over a slot, which will allow the door to be adjusted away from the cabinet if the door is 'binding' (rubbing) **[a]**.

The second type of adjustment is made by tightening or loosening the smaller fixed screw, located next to the first screw mentioned above. This adjusts the door to the left or right of the cabinet (as you look at it) when closed, allowing you to centralize and position the doors equally apart **[b]**.

The third area of adjustment is on the hinge plate that's attached to the cabinet. This plate has a vertical slot, which allows the door to be raised or lowered to align with the cabinet and the other doors **[c]**. All three adjustments are easily made with nothing more than a cross-head (Phillips) screwdriver.

To adjust an entire drawer (not just the drawer front), first remove the drawer from the unit by pulling it right out, then lift the front of the drawer to free the drawer from the runners **[d]**.

Make a few pencil marks on the unit to show the existing position and the proposed new position. Unscrew the runners and reposition them **[e]**. Use a cramp to hold the runner in position temporarily, to allow for new pilot holes to be drilled **[f]**, before securing with screws.

If the drawer slides perfectly in its runners but its front rubs on a door or worktop as it closes, you may be able to solve the problem by simply unscrewing the front from the drawer, repositioning the drawer front and screwing it back together again **[g]**.

Replacing kitchen cupboard doors

One quick and easy way to give your kitchen a highly noticeable makeover is to replace the cupboard doors. Many units are built to standard sizes and a wide range of different designs and styles of replacement doors is now available.

Using a slotted or crosshead screwdriver, undo the door hinges, leaving in place the hinge plates that are attached to the unit **[a]**. The replacement doors normally have their hinge holes pre-cut. If not, the holes can be cut quite easily using a circular hinge-cutter, which simply fits into the end of your drill.

Replacement hinges are readily available from DIY stores and hardware shops. Transfer the hinges from the old door, and fit them to the new door with the two fixing screws **[b]**. Use a bradawl to start the screw holes.

Tools required
Screwdriver
Tape measure
Square
Drill
Wood bits
Cramp
Circular hinge-cutter
Bradawl

Hold the new door up to the unit, and screw the hinge in place on the hinge plate via the large central screw **[c]**. The second screw is for adjustment only, in order to align the door to the unit. Repeat this process for the bottom hinge.

Replace the door handles by marking their positions and drilling through to attach the

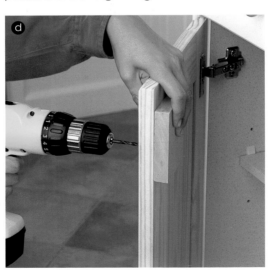

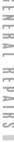

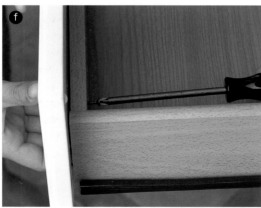

handles. To avoid breakout occurring when you drill through the door, temporarily attach a block of wood to the door behind the drilling point with a cramp **[d]** (see bottom, page 91).

Next, simply hold the handle and screw in the threaded bolt **[e]**. If the bolt is a little too short, countersink the hole on the inside of the door to allow the bolt to protrude a little further out from the front surface of the door.

Replacing kitchen drawer fronts is a very simple process. Firstly, remove the old drawer

front by undoing the two retaining screws located inside the drawer **[f]**.
Attach the new drawer handle, by drilling holes through the centre of the
drawer front **[g]**. Countersink the hole a little bit on the back of the drawer
front to prevent the bolt head from protruding out of the edge of the
drawer when it has been attached.

Attach the new drawer front by screwing through the two fixing points,
into the back face of each of the drawer fronts **[h]**. Repeat this process
on all the units. Once you have completed the job, replacing all the doors
and drawer fronts, decorate the new surfaces to your taste to complete
the transformation of your kitchen. If you find that any of the new doors or
drawers rub or stick, make adjustments as necessary.

GENERAL REPAIRS

Repairing/overhauling doors

Household doors get a lot of use and take a bashing, especially when there are children living in the house. For this reason they tend to need more maintenance than most household items. Basic repairs are relatively easy to effect.

Sticking doors

With the onset of winter and damp conditions, doors may possibly start to stick along their sides and bottoms and might need 'easing'. However, before you do any remedial work, first check that the hinges are not worn or broken. If the door rocks a bit when pushed and pulled, this is normally a sign that the hinges are worn. In this case, replace them immediately.

Firstly, we will consider a side-sticking door, with sound hinges. Close the door tightly and mark a pencil line down the edge against the jamb **[a]**. You will see where the door needs easing back from the high points along the pencil line. Use a hand plane to plane off the high points until the edge is the same distance from the pencil line all the way down **[b]**.

> **MUST KNOW**
>
> **Tools required**
> Plane
> Pencil
> Hammer
> Chisel
> Screwdriver

WATCH OUT!

Plane stupid
In the case of a badly sticking door, don't be tempted to plane too vigorously. If so, you might leave a very unsightly outside edge.

Shut the door once more and, using a flat piece of wood – a piece of hardboard will do – scribe a line on the bottom of the door **[c]**. This will show where you have any tight points on the floor. Remove the door from its hinges and plane off any points.

In some instances you may have to adjust the hinges on the door in order to square it to the frame for a good fit. Alternatively, you may need to pack the hinges out if they have been cut in too deep, which might make the door bind on the frame. These tasks will involve actually removing the door and holding it in position as you work on it, so it may be advisable to ask someone to help you, as doors tend to be heavy and awkward. If you are working alone,

remove the door and hinges **[d]**, and wedge the door underneath with small wedges to support it in the open position. Now cut small packers from thin card **[e]**, place the card packers behind the hinges **[f]** and then screw them back into position. This will adjust your door towards the jamb. You may need one or two pieces of card, depending on the amount of adjustment required. Screw the hinge(s) back into position, replacing only one screw per hinge as you close the door to check for fit. Add or remove pieces of card until you have the right combination for a perfect square fit and no binding, then fix the rest of the screws into the hinges.

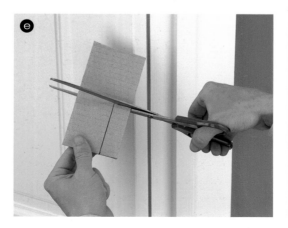

MUST KNOW

Hole in one
If you fiddle with the hinges of a door too much, ultimately you will enlarge the screw holes by constantly removing and replacing the hinge screws. This is turn will lead to the door hinges slipping in the jamb, which will see a return to your original problem of a sticking door. Try to get your adjustments right in one go.

If you have a rattling door, this means the door is not meeting the stop or jamb correctly, in which case you will need to remove and replace the jamb in a new position for a good fit.

Take a hammer and chisel and gently tap the joint between jamb and frame to ease the jamb off, using a piece of wood to lever against and ease the jamb away from the frame (this prevents any damage caused by the lever). Remove all nails or just hammer back to the face of the wood for re-fixing. Now close the door. Re-fix the vertical jamb first to allow the door to close firmly but tightly **[g]** and then the other vertical jamb followed by the top jamb for a perfect rattle-free door.

Strengthening a hinge

Quite often a common problem occurs when a door has been taken off and re-fixed a few times. The screws loosen within the fixing holes, and the door doesn't operate properly (this can also be a cause of a door sticking or binding). The problem is simply solved by paring down some softwood into dowels. Add PVA wood glue and tap the dowels into the old holes. When the glue has gone off, cut off the excess dowel and re-fix the hinges.

Replacing door furniture

If you want to freshen up the look of your house, one quick way to do this after basic re-decoration is to replace the door furniture throughout. You will be spoilt for choice for handles and other items – some shops sell them exclusively.

Replacing a door handle

Begin by removing the old door handle. Using a screwdriver, remove the four screws holding the handle plate **[a]**. Remember to remove only one side of the handle plate at a time. Then, place the new handle over the square spindle **[b]** to check if you need to cut the spindle shorter, in order to allow the new handle plate to sit flat against the door when it has been fitted.

Use the spirit level to check if your new handle plate is level by holding it vertically against the edge of the fitting. Then mark your fixing holes with a bradawl **[c]** and drill small pilot holes for the screws **[d]**. Make sure the holes are just big enough to accept the screw provided with the new handles. Screw the first handle to the door checking with the spirit level **[e]** and adjusting as you go **[f]**. Now go to the other side of the door and do exactly the same to fix the other handle.

Oiling the latch mechanism

You should oil your door latch mechanisms regularly in order to ensure their continued trouble-free operation. To do this, remove both door handles and the spindle, remembering to place something on the floor between the door and the jamb to keep the door ajar. Use a cushion or something else soft to wedge the door open, so that its decor will not be damaged.

Place a long bladed screwdriver through the hole where the spindle goes, and remove the two holding screws.

Holding the screwdriver either side of the door, give it a firm pull towards the forward edge to free the latch **[g]**. Having oiled the latch, push it back into position and replace the two fixing screws. Replace the handles as mentioned above.

MUST KNOW

Tools required
Small screwdriver
Small spirit level
Bradawl
Drill

Door security

You can save a lot of money by making your home properly secure yourself, rather than paying professionals to do the job. Good home security begins with good door security.

Fitting hinge bolts and door guards

Fitting hinge bolts is a relatively straightforward job. It is a good idea to fit at least two bolts per door, as quite simply the more you have, the more secure your door will be. Open the door and drill a hole on the inside of the door large enough to accommodate the bolt **[a]**. Mark a point on the frame directly in line with the bolt hole and drill another hole. This is where the locking plate will be situated. Recess the locking plate into the frame and screw it in place **[b]**.

Fitting a door guard is also an easy job, with no special skill required, as the components are all face fixed. Place the door guard a few inches above the door handle and position the receiving bracket on the doorframe. Mark, pilot drill **[c]** and screw fix. The fixing plate may have to be recessed to finish flush with the door. Position the bolt arm on the door, mark, pilot drill and screw fix **[d]**. Check that the alignment of

the bolt arm and receiving bracket is correct **[e]** and then make any adjustments as necessary.

Fitting good locks and bolts to all exterior doors is essential for good home security. Cheap locks are a poor buy, but good locks poorly fitted are not much better than useless. Bolts are very good for security, but are obviously only useable when you are at home, as they are applied from within.

Basic minimum recommendations for good door security would be a deadlocking cylinder rim lock fitted about a third of the way down from the door top and a mortise lock fitted about a third up from the bottom. It might be a good idea also to have a second mortise lock fitted to the central door rail, lockable with matching keys to the bottom mortise lock. (Your local locksmiths can easily match a second lock to the first.) You could also fit a third hinge centrally if the door only has two, as this will strengthen the whole door and reduce the likelihood of it being smashed in on its hinged side.

Packing out door bolts sometimes become necessary if there has been movement or expansion in the door. Unscrew and remove the catch plate on the frame **[f]**. Pack it out with small pieces of card until you get the correct alignment of the bolt and catch plate **[g]**. Screw back into place and make a final check for fit.

Repairing/overhauling windows

Window frames bear the brunt of bad weather and as a result need regular maintenance. This is especially the case if the window frames are made of wood.

The most commonly used window is the type known as a casement window. This design of window is particularly vulnerable to the weather, simply because casement windows are normally face fixed (flush with the brickwork) and thus have no protection from the weather. The opening sash often distorts slightly with the weather, causing it to rattle and become draughty. One simple solution may be to move the catch plate of the lever fastener, to pull the sash tighter into the frame so preventing the

rattle and reducing the draught.

Undo the catch plate from its original position on the mullion or transom and move it slightly away from the sash **[a]**. Hold the catch plate in its new position, use a bradawl to start off the new fixing holes **[b]**, insert the screws and secure. Having moved the catch plate slightly, when the window is closed, the rattle should hopefully now be eradicated.

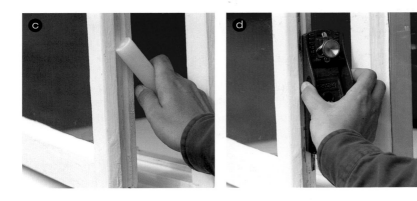

Windows can tend to stick after a while, particularly if they are left undecorated. A window will quickly let in moisture, which will make the timber swell, in turn making the window difficult to open and close. When a window sticks, a lot of people force the window either open or shut. Be careful when doing this, as forcing the window can break the mortice and tenon joints, if it is of 'sash-style' construction ie. a frame containing panes.

To resolve the problem, use candle wax on both the frame's window edge and the mullion or transom edge **[c]**. If that does not work, you may need to plane the edge of the sash to allow the window to operate efficiently **[d]**. Keep attempting to open and close the window whilst planing, to ensure that you remove only the minimum amount necessary.

After planing the edge, it is very important to paint the raw edge with primer, undercoat and a topcoat of exterior paint as soon as possible **[e]**. Allow the paint to dry fully between coats, and then shine it with wax.

MUST KNOW

Tools required
Screwdriver
Bradawl
Hammer
Craft knife
Plane
Sandpaper
Candle wax

Replacing panes of glass

If a pane of window glass breaks you could call the glazier, but it is actually a straightforward job to make a replacement yourself. Wear gloves for this job, to avoid cuts to your hands.

Replacing the glass from a beaded window

As well as working gloves, it is a good idea to put on protective eyewear before you proceed. Starting from the top of the broken pane, use a hammer and chisel to gently lever out the beads from the frame. Be sure to remove all of the glass, piece by piece, as you go around the frame **[a]**.

When you have removed all the broken glass, clean any existing compound off the window frame. Now measure the inside of the frame and have the new pane cut 3mm (⅛in) smaller on each dimension to allow tolerance when fitting.

Run a bead of compound around the inside of the frame to seal the glass and frame. Place the lower edge of the pane on to the bottom rebate of the frame and press the pane carefully into place **[b]**. Fix the top bead first by lightly tapping the pins into place, following them with the bottom bead, and finally the side beads **[c]**. You can now drive the pins home using the nail set punch. Fill and sand any holes before retouching the paintwork.

Replacing the glass from a puttied window

Again wearing thick working gloves and protective glasses, remove the broken windowpane. You may need to use strips of sticking tape to hold any broken pieces in place **[d]**.

Using the glazier's hacking knife and hammer, carefully chip away the putty from the frame **[e]**. Starting from the top, work each piece free as you go around, also pulling out any sprigs you come across with the pincers. Clean off all remnants of old putty and seal the frame with wood primer.

Using a ball of putty the size of the palm of your hand, press a thin line of putty along the inside of the frames **[f]**. The bed for the glass to press/seal against should be about 3mm (⅛in) thick.

Lower the bottom edge of the glass into the rebate of the frame **[g]**. Press all around and secure in place using the glazing sprigs. Tap the sprigs into the frame using the edge of a chisel so they lie flat against the glass. Trim the surplus putty from the inside of the frame with the putty knife **[h]**. Now apply an even but thick layer of putty to the outside of the frame and with the putty knife work the putty to a smooth 45° band. Trim any excess putty and paint when dry.

Window security

Good window security is possibly even more important than that for exterior doors, given that many windows are so easy to break and enter. Many different precautions can be taken.

Changing an existing casement fastener for a lockable handle

Begin this job by removing the existing handle and catch. Use a screwdriver for this and take care not to slip and damage the wood. It may be necessary to fill one or two of the holes with filler, as there is a good chance that the new handle and catch will probably not match the existing fixing holes.

Hold the new catch up to the fixed part of the window in the same location as the old one. Using the bradawl, press into the wood, twisting as you go through the holes in the catch **[a]**. Doing this will create small pilot holes for the fixing screws. Next, screw the catch firmly to the window frame **[b]**.

To fix the lockable handle to the opening casement side, mark your holes and place the handle over the catch. Close the window, wedging it with paper, and mark the holes. Now

GENERAL REPAIRS

106

use the bradawl to make the pilot holes as before and finally screw the handle to the casement window **[c]**.

Fixing a swing lock

This type of lock is also an ideal replacement for a standard fastener. It is a neat, unobtrusive little lock, which is usually supplied in a white powder coated finish. The lock is fitted by exactly the same method as that for the lockable handle fastener; screw the plate to the window frame **[d]**; use a bradawl to make fixing holes for the catch on the window **[e]**; check alignment and screw the catch onto the window **[f]**. Keep the lock functioning perfectly by lubricating it occasionally with light oil.

Draughtproofing windows & doors

Preventing draughts from getting past doors and windows and into the house will save you money and ensure your family's comfort. Draughtproofing is quick and easy to effect.

Windows

Most hinged casement windows made of wood will at some time warp and become ill-fitting, causing draughts and discomfort. This problem can easily be eradicated using a soft plastic, self-adhesive moulded draught excluder.

Basic draught excluder usually comes in a double width roll, which you will need to split into two single strips for windows **[a]**. Make sure the surfaces are clean. Starting at one end, peel off the backing paper of the strip to reveal the adhesive side **[b]**. This will be stuck to the outside of the fixed window frames, which the opening casement will press against when closed.

Working from the top of the right hand corner, carefully press the end of the excluder into place, leaving a 25mm (1in) trimming edge **[c]**. Work anti-clockwise around the edge of the frame. Cut the ends of each length at a 45° angle to form a neat joint at each corner. Close

MUST KNOW

Tools required
Small screwdriver
Bradawl
Scissors
Saw (optional)

the window and secure it firmly in place to enable the excluder to stick properly.

Doors

Doorframes can be draughtproofed using the double draught excluder applied as described above. Another source of draughts in doors is the keyhole. This problem can be solved by fixing what is known as an escutcheon plate over the keyhole **[d]**.

Another place vulnerable to draughts is the front door letterbox opening. You can purchase ready-made brush draught excluders, but be sure to have the dimensions of your letterbox with you when you go shopping. A little oversize

is all right, but undersize will not work at all. Before you begin, remove the inside flap of the letterbox if you have one, as the brush excluder will be replacing this.

Place the brush frame over the letterbox, opening on the inside of the door. Make sure the frame is squarely over the opening, mark the holes with the bradawl and then screw the draught excluder securely to the door **[e]**.

It really is worthwhile spending some time and money draught-proofing your home properly: the benefits are immense.

▶ Insulating lofts

Loft insulation is the biggest single cost-saving improvement you can make to your home. Rolls of insulation blanket can be bought inexpensively from any DIY store and are easy to install.

There are two main types of insulation – blanket (which comes in rolls) or loose fill (supplied in bags). The most common form of insulation is the blanket type. The recommended minimum depth of insulation is 150mm (6in), but the more the better: 25 to 30 per cent of heat loss occurs through un-insulated roofs.

Ideally, work off a couple of short scaffold boards laid across the joists of your loft. If you do not have a permanent light in your loft, use a lead light hung up at a high vantage point. Bring all the insulation into the loft space but don't open any of the rolls until you are actually ready to fit out the loft. When packed, the insulation is compressed, so when it is rolled out between the joists, it will expand a little. The rolls measure approximately 39–41cm (15–16in) wide x 7.5m (25ft) long. Trim the ends in a chamfer shape to allow airflow from the eaves, then begin rolling out the insulation blanket **[a]**. Try to ensure that electrical cables aren't covered by the insulation. Lift the cables and roll the insulation underneath **[b]**. This will

avoid any overheating of the cables. Also ensure that any light casings or lamp fittings protruding into the loft are not covered. Trim closely around these with an extended craft knife or

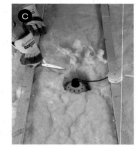

sharp kitchen scissors **[c]**. Beware of cutting any cables! To make doubly sure none of the heat escapes from your property, lay a second layer of insulation at right angles to the first and cover right over the joists **[d]**. The procedure is the same as that for the first layer, as are the precautions.

If you are using loose fill insulation, it is very important to cut strips of plywood or hardboard fixed between the joists to form a barrier and keep the eaves clear **[e]**. The depth of fill necessary is approximately 15cm (6in) – you may need to raise the height of the joists by attaching battens, thus allowing boarding to be laid down for walking on in your loft.

Pour in the insulation fill **[f]** and spread with a timber or plywood off-cut. Tamp down and level the insulation fill so that it lies evenly between the joists **[g]**.

want to know **more?**

Take it to the next level...

Go to...
▶ **Painting** – pages 28–31
▶ **Insulating pipes** – pages 130–1
▶ **Making trellis** – pages 160–3

Other sources
▶ **Adult education classes**
investigate whether your local authority provides a home maintenance course
▶ **DIY clubs**
look through your local paper and meet up with other enthusiastic amateurs
▶ **Websites**
visit www.askthebuilder.com
▶ **Books**
Collins Complete DIY Manual

plumbing

jobs

Many plumbing jobs require special skills and should really only be attempted by a professional or an advanced DIY-er. However, there are a number of tasks that can be undertaken by anyone with basic DIY skills that will save both time and money.

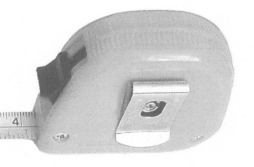

Connecting a washing machine

Many homes have washing machines these days and it seems a shame to have to call out a plumber to perform a task as basic as connecting one to the water supply.

Begin by reading and thoroughly familiarising yourself with the manufacturer's instructions that come with the washing machine. Check that wherever you are going to install the machine, the water pressure level will be high enough to run it satisfactorily. To get the best performance from your washing machine, always ensure that the machine is positioned both level and plumb.

When you buy a new washing machine, it will come with two inlet hoses – blue for the cold water supply and red for the hot water. These hoses are connected to the outlets on the back of the machine **[a]**, via colour coded washing machine valves attached to the water supply **[b]**.

Some machines have only a cold supply with just one hose, in which case the fitting procedure is exactly the same as for a machine with a dual water supply. However, it is far more expensive to run this type of machine, because the water has to be heated in the machine.

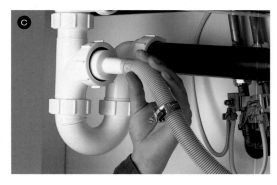

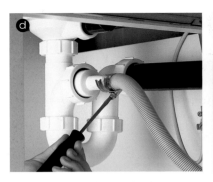

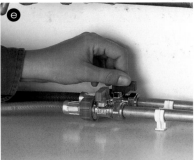

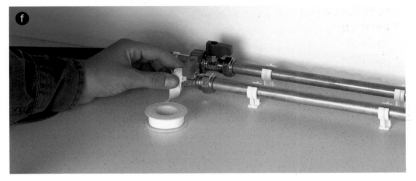

The hook-shaped waste hose is fitted into a 40mm (1⅝in) vertical plastic waste pipe attached to a deep seal trap and away to a gully. The hose is loosely fitted into the standpipe to avoid dirty water being siphoned back into the machine. Ensure that the pipe is a minimum of 610mm (24in) in height from the floor **[c]**.

Some sink waste traps have a spigot end to attach a washing machine. Make sure you fit an in-line anti-siphon return valve, to avoid dirty water returning into the machine. The valve fits in the machine outlet hose simply with a hose connector at each end **[d]**.

Don't forget to turn on the power and the valves before you slide the machine into place **[e]**. If you spot a slight leak on the valve connection, wrap some PTFE tape around the thread **[f]** and reconnect the fittings.

WATCH OUT!

Level and plumb
Don't be tempted to run your washing machine without it being properly level. It will vibrate, make a loud noise and soon become damaged.

Clearing airlocks

Airlocks are common in household plumbing systems, particularly in older properties or wherever there are runs of pipes which are not straight. They are normally easy to clear.

When an airlock occurs, it often appears as a spluttering and hissing tap. The air needs to be forced out, which is normally best achieved by working on the kitchen sink, where the water in the plumbing system generally starts. Take a piece of rubber hose – slip one end over the spout of the kitchen mixer tap **[a]**, and the other end over the spout of the bathroom basin hot tap **[b]**. Turn the cold tap on the kitchen mixer tap wide open **[c]**, then turn the hot tap on the basin wide open **[d]**, which will force the air through the bathroom hot tap by using mains pressure until the water is flowing freely.

To clear the bath taps, repeat this process by closing the basin tap, and if necessary the tank supply, by closing the hand basin hot tap, forcing the air bubbles into the tank. The whole line is now clear.

If you have a mixer tap in the kitchen, remove the spout and hold your hand tightly over the opening. Fully open the hot tap and slowly open the cold and force the air up through the open bath tap.

Another common cause of airlocks is if the water mains supply is turned off and the tank is emptied. To fix the problem, use the same method as described above.

Air trapped in a radiator is easily detected by touch. If only half the radiator is hot, you probably have an air pocket trapped within the radiator, which will affect its efficiency. There is a small bleed valve on the top left or right corner

Tools required
Piece of rubber hose
Radiator valve key
Dry cloth

of the radiator. You will need a radiator key to open this valve. Push the radiator bleeding key onto the valve **[e]** and turn it gently to release the trapped air. You will hear a hissing sound, until water begins to squirt out. When this happens, immediately shut off the bleed valve. Be prepared, and have some old rags on hand to soak up any spillage **[f]**.

Check the water pressure indicator on your combi boiler. If the pressure is low and needs topping up, carefully open up the screw on the valve in the filling loop at the bottom of the boiler **[g]**, using a slotted screwdriver if necessary. Watch the water pressure indicator and shut off the feed immediately by turning back the valve screw when the correct pressure has been reached.

Fitting thermostatic valves

Thermostatic valves are a useful innovation in any house with central heating as they enable you to control the ambient temperature room-by-room. They are easy to fit.

Firstly, drain down the system by shutting off the boiler. Leave for a while to allow the water to cool, then switch off the supply to the expansion tank via the stopcock. Next, slip one end of a length of garden hose over the drain cock, the other end into the gully. Open the drain cock with a key or adjustable spanner and release all the water. Any water trapped in the heating system can be removed by opening the bleed valves on all the radiators, starting at the furthest from the drain cock. Pack some dry cloths around the pipe under the old valve. Hold the main body of the valve with a set of grips and, using an adjustable spanner, undo the radiator union nut **[a]**. Use the same method to remove the cap nut from the bottom of the valve **[b]**. Remove the old valve **[c]**.

Removing the cap nut and olive can be difficult. If the olive is brass (yellowish) it can be removed with care, freeing the cap nut **[d]**. A

MUST KNOW

Tools required
Adjustable spanner
Plumber's
  grips/wrench
Radiator valve
  spanner
Pipe cutter
Dry cloths

copper olive (same colour as pipe) would have compressed onto the pipe when tightened, so in this case it is necessary to cut the olive off with pipe cutters. Some thermostatic valves may be longer or shorter than the original, requiring some alteration to the pipe work.

Slide on the cap nut and then the new olive **[e]**. Older valves might have different tails from new thermostatic valves, so it is important to compare the originals with the tail supplied with the new valve. If they are different, fit the new tail into the radiator by using a radiator valve spanner, which is basically a large Allen key.

Wrap PTFE tape (see Glossary for explanation) around the thread half a dozen times or so before fitting for a really sound joint.

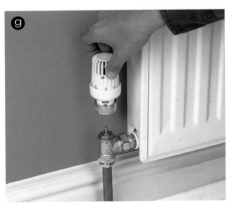

Half-tighten the valve to the union first, then the cap nut **[f]**. Once aligned, tighten the union first, then finish tightening the cap nut **[g]**.

Originally, thermostatic valves had to be fitted on the radiator flow side (ingoing) but now modern thermostatic valves are bi-directional, so the valve can be fitted on either side of the radiator.

Curing a dripping tap

A dripping tap wastes water and, if left long enough, will damage the porcelain or aluminium of basins, baths and sinks. This is generally not a difficult problem to solve.

There may be a few different reasons for a dripping tap, but all are fairly simple to solve. Mixer taps on the kitchen sink are very commonplace today, so this is the kind of tap you are most likely to encounter.

Before you begin, remember to turn OFF the water supply. If the tap is leaking from the base of the spout, remove the spout **[a]**, prise off the circlip at its base and check the washer at the base of the spout for wear and tear **[b]**. Replace the washer if necessary.

Next, prise off the head cover of the tap itself **[c]**. You will need to remove the shrouded head from the tap to expose the retaining screw. If there is no screw, the head will just pull off, exposing the spindle **[d]**. Use an adjustable spanner to remove the spindle headgear **[e]**.

Then remove the spindle itself **[f]**.

There are normally two O-rings, which when worn leak water from the top of the tap shroud. There is also a rubber tap washer at the bottom of the headgear, held on with a nut. Undo

and replace this washer **[g]** if the tap is dripping from the spout.

There are more O-ring seals on a swivel spout. If water seeps out on the swivel, these O-ring seals need replacing. Undo the small grub screw and pop out the swivel spout and replace the seals.

If the headgear is all seized up and corroded, purchase a headgear replacement kit. Take the tap headgear with you when you buy any replacements.

If you have ceramic disc taps, then these are supposed to be maintenance-free, but problems can still occur. Even though there are no washers to replace on ceramic disc taps, if they need repairing you will have to renew the inner cartridge as a whole. Remove the headgear from the tap body and replace any worn parts.

Changing the taps on a bath

Mixer taps with built-in shower attachments offer an extra dimension to baths, so if you have old fashioned individual taps it might be worth considering changing them over.

Whenever you are planning on changing any key element in your bathroom – from the basic suite to the taps or other accessories – it is worth thinking very hard about what you really want, because the choice on offer is absolutely vast. For example, if you are somebody who likes to change their decor on a regular basis, a classic white suite with chrome fittings is probably a better idea than a coloured suite, which might date or clash with subsequent changes you make to your bathroom.

Butler kitchen sinks have enjoyed a renaissance in recent times and look superb with a high quality set of mixer taps, regardless of whether the sink and taps are renovated originals or reproductions. However, you don't need to go to such trouble or expense – even a basic stainless steel sink will benefit from a change of taps.

MUST KNOW

Tools required
Slotted screwdriver
Wrench

Changing a tap

Turn off the isolator valve beneath the tap with a slotted screwdriver **[a]**; otherwise, turn off your

mains stopcock and drain down the system by opening the taps.

Undo the pipe work and waste connections beneath the bath or sink's taps [b]. Unscrew the back nut using a wrench [c] and lift out the old taps [d]. This is a good opportunity to clean the area thoroughly around the taps before refitting the new taps or mixer unit. This area is often prone to a build-up of unsightly scale.

Insert the new taps or mixer into position onto plastic or rubber washers to protect the sink and seal from leaks [e], press the unit firmly home [f], and then connect the pipes to the base of the taps beneath the bath [g]. The distance between the centres of tap holes on sinks and baths is generally between 175–180mm (7–7¼in). Having said that, there are swivel union attachments that can be added to allow a lot more tolerance.

Make sure you fit the flat rubber washer and hand-tighten the shower hose [h], if there is one. Ideally, give the hose a half turn with the wrench, but use a cloth to avoid any scratching.

Take this opportunity to fit some flexible copper pipe to the tap tails to enable easier fitting and maintenance – this will mean some small adjustments to the pipe work.

The procedure for a sink mixer is as above, but you might be able to remove the sink for ease of fitting as you change the taps.

WATCH OUT!

Not too tight
Be careful when tightening up any plumbing joint. Too many turns with a wrench and you could end up breaking the joint.

Changing the washer on your ballcock

If you have water pouring out of your overflow pipe or there is constant noise from your cold water tank or toilet cistern, the chances are that a ballcock washer needs changing.

Changing the washer on a water tank

Shut off the water supply to the loft storage tank by turning off the stopcock. Then drain off the tank water by opening the bathroom taps. Take out the split pin from the valve, which will in turn release the float arm. Unscrew the cap at the end of the float valve, pop out the piston from the body and unscrew the piston end cap. Stop the piston rotating by inserting a slotted screwdriver into the gap. Remove all the remains of the old washer and clean the cap out with a wire wool pad and fit in the new washer. Lubricate the new washer with a touch of silicone grease. Connect the float arm to the valve, re-fix the split pin and turn the water back on. See the box below for essential information about the different types of valve.

MUST KNOW

Tools required
Plumber's grips
Bradawl
Slotted screwdriver
Wire wool pad
Silicone grease

MUST KNOW

How valves work
The Portsmouth valve has a solid brass rod float arm with a float attached to the end. Bending the rod downwards slightly forces the float down and cuts off the valve earlier, letting less water into the tank. Bending the rod upwards opens the valve longer and allows more water into the tank. On a diaphragm valve, there is a screw on the float arm, which when turned towards the valve, lowers the water level or when turned away allows more water into the tank.

Changing the washer on a toilet

To turn off the water supply to the toilet cistern, without interfering with the supply to the rest of the house, use a slotted screwdriver to turn the isolator valve screw **[a]**. Once you have done this, drain down the cistern by flushing the toilet.

Undo the top of the valve with the arm and float connected and set them aside **[b]**. Next, unscrew the ball valve assembly and remove the plastic piston **[c]**.

Remove the old washer, ensuring that any remaining residue around the washer is carefully removed, using the pad of wire wool **[d]**. Fit the new washer and lubricate it with a touch of silicone grease.

Fit all the components of the cistern back together again, turn the water back on and try flushing the toilet. Hopefully, everything will work properly. If not, take everything apart once more and try the whole procedure again.

Clearing blocked drains & toilets

This is not an especially pleasant DIY job to undertake, but it helps to know what to do in an emergency – which is so often the case – and saves the cost of calling out a plumber.

In order to clear the kitchen sink, first try using a spoonful or two of caustic soda **[a]**, applying it directly down the plughole, and if that doesn't work, use a plunger. Place a cloth in the overflow then pump the plunger up and down over the waste outlet **[b]**. Repeat the process until the blockage clears. If the blockage remains, you should undo the trap under the sink **[c]** and try clearing that.

MUST KNOW

Tools required
Plunger
Auger
Wire coat hanger
Protective clothing
Disinfectant and soap

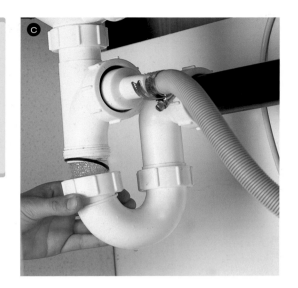

WATCH OUT!

Bucket required
Place a bucket or
washing up bowl
beneath the sink
trap whenever you
open it. There will
always be a flood of
waste water.

If the toilet is not flushing properly, this would
suggest that a blockage has already formed.
Deal with this problem immediately, or the
lavatory might overflow at any time.

One simple and efficient way to remove a
blockage from a toilet is to take a black rubbish
bag, roll your sleeves right up and put your arm
deep into the bag. Lower your bag-wrapped
arm into the toilet and grab whatever is causing
the blockage. As you withdraw your arm, allow
the bag to close itself around the item. This
way the obstruction is removed, your arm
remains dry, and you need not see the
offending article.

A larger version of the kitchen plunger is also
available for hire for clearing toilets. In this case,
you push the plunger down into the toilet U-
bend and pump. If this works, the water level
will drop quickly and the WC will make a
gurgling sound. Rinse with hot water and
disinfectant to clean.

If the blockage remains after using the basic
methods for unblocking described above, hire a

WC auger **[d]**. This is a flexible cable, which should be pushed as far as possible into the U-bend **[e]**, with the handle then being cranked to unblock the toilet. Again, when you have finished, rinse with hot water and disinfect.

Before you start any of the major internal operations explained above, it is a good idea to lift up the manhole cover in the garden or street if possible, to check whether or not that is blocked.

Hire a set of drain rods, or borrow some from a friend. Screw two rods together with a plunger or corkscrew top at the head **[f]**; slide this into the drain run, going with the flow of the waste water. Add another rod each time it becomes necessary and push the assembled line of rods to and fro, further into the drain **[g]**. It helps if you also have a hose running into the manhole to help flush the blockage through.

If the manhole is not blocked, it may be that the soil stack pipe is blocked instead. Undo a rodding eye on the stack using a hired auger to clear the blockage.

WATCH OUT!

Hygiene matters
Unblocking drains and toilets can be unpleasant, smelly work. Pay great attention to hygiene at all times – best to wear gloves.

Blocked gullies are easily cleared. Raise the grille and put your hand into the gully – always wearing rubber gloves – and remove any debris from the trap **[h]**. Ensure the outlet from the gully is also clear. Rinse the gully with the hose and clean with suitable cleaner.

If any of the procedures described above fail, it is vital to call out a professional to ascertain the cause of the blockage and correct it as soon as possible. This is particularly important in the case of blocked gullies running down into main drains, as if the blockage is not relieved promptly it could cause problems further down the line which might affect neighbours and other people living in the vicinity.

Professionals who specialise in unblocking drains can charge exorbitant fees for a difficult job, so be sure to get an accurate quotation before they embark on the job. However, having said that, they are equipped with specialist devices such as cameras on flexible rods which can identify the cause of major problems and provide solutions far more quickly than an amateur.

Insulating/lagging tanks & pipes

Protecting pipes and water tanks with lagging is a worthwhile undertaking that will save you money and possibly prevent the catastrophe of winter-frozen pipes.

Lagging a cold water tank

To lag a cold water tank, the easiest method is to buy a purpose made 'insulation jacket', which is fibre glass wadding inside a plastic covering, normally with its own fixing ties. Securing one of these to the tank is usually pretty straightforward.

If you do not wish to purchase a ready-made insulation jacket, it is possible to make your own by cutting pieces of hardboard to match all four sides of the tank (as well as its lid). Cut some roof insulation and stick it to the hardboard by painting PVA adhesive on with a brush and placing the insulating material directly on top of the glue. Alternatively, you could just place a cut-down piece of insulating material in a black plastic sack and make a blanket that way **[a]**. Secure the panels or blankets in place around the tank with string **[b]**.

Whenever you are working in the loft, ensure that you place a short scaffold board or similar across the joists, to avoid accidents and damage to the ceilings.

Insulating pipework

Pipe insulation is very simple to fit. There is a felt-sock type of material on a roll that you slide over the pipe, normally fitted when the pipes are actually being installed in the first place, and more often used under floors and screeds, or the foam type, which comes in long lengths and is usually pre-split along its length for easy

MUST KNOW

Tools required
Craft knife
Sharp kitchen knife
Saw
Paint brush
Adjustable square

installation. The latter is much better for fitting to pipes which are already in position.

Cut the tubes to length with a craft knife. Open the tube by the split and slide it over the pipe **[c]**. Abut straight joints and use insulating tape to seal the joints **[d]**.

A right or left hand bend requires a mitre cut. Using an adjustable square, mark the 45° angle and cut the tube to length. Repeat the process in the other direction to complete the angle **[e]**, press the two angled ends of the insulating material together to make the joint **[f]**, and tape the join with insulating tape.

To make a tee joint, cut a 90°-angled cut to half-depth on a straight length of insulating sock, and then cut a matching shape to fit snugly against this **[g]**. Complete the joint by taping the pieces together with insulating tape.

Insulating around a bend in the pipe work is achieved by cutting a series of V-shaped cuts on the one side of the tube, bending it to the shape of the bend as you squeeze the tube onto the pipe **[h]**, and then sealing the cuts and joints with insulating tape in order to hold all the pieces firmly in place.

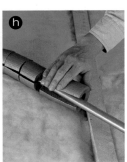

want to know more?

Take it to the next level...

Go to...
▶ **Insulating lofts** – pages 110–11
▶ **External water tap** – pages 176–7
▶ **Routine checks** – pages 14–17

Other sources
▶ **Finding a skilled plumber**
  The Institute of Plumbing and Heating Engineering (IPHE) has a directory on its website: www.iphe.org.uk
▶ **Local DIY stores**
  ask advice on buying the correct tools
▶ **Part-time course**
  get an NVQ at your local college
▶ **Books**
  Collins Plumbing and Central Heating

electrical

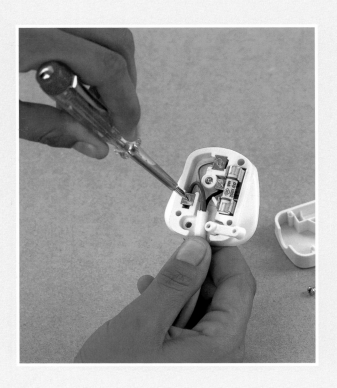

work

Like plumbing, electrical work
is at the more challenging end
of the DIY spectrum. Electricity
is very dangerous unless dealt
with by experienced hands,
but nevertheless there are
a number of basic jobs that
any DIY-er can undertake
with complete confidence.

Installing a doorbell

This is one of those DIY jobs that anyone with basic skills should aspire to do. It seems a shame to hire a professional to do a job that requires only the most basic knowledge of electricity and the most simple usage of tools and materials.

Installing a wind-up doorbell

The easiest type of doorbells to install are the wind-up models, which require no wiring for electricity. They operate by being wound up, and as the button connected to them is pressed, this releases the spring and causes the striker to hit the bell. The downside of this type of doorbell is that they need to be wound up frequently. However, care should be taken not to over-wind them as they can then become jammed and will not work properly.

To fit a wind-up doorbell, drill a hole through the door from the outside and push the shaft from the button through to the inside of the door **[a]**. Screw the button to the outside of the door. On the inside of the door, place the bottom of the bell over the shaft and screw this firmly into place **[b]**. Replace the outer cover of the doorbell and wind up the mechanism **[c]**. Your doorbell is ready for operation.

> **MUST KNOW**
>
> **Tools required**
> Drill and bit
> Screwdriver
> Electrical screwdriver
> Hammer
> Cable cutter
> Cable dips

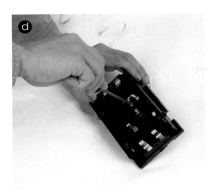

Installing a battery operated doorbell

You can install a battery operated doorbell system anywhere near the door, but make sure that you do not situate the unit near a heat source. The battery housing will normally be located within the bell casing, with two terminals for joining to the other end of the wires coming from the doorbell button. It does not make any difference which way round you connect the wires to the terminals – either way is fine **[d]**.

Drill a hole through the doorframe for the wire. Fix the battery box to the wall above the door **[e]**, run the wire down the side of the frame and thread it through the hole to the other side. Put the cover of the unit back on **[f]**. Gently hammer in the cable clips to secure the cable neatly to the frame **[g]**. Separate the conductors and join each one to the end of the bell terminal **[h]**. Screw the button fixing into place.

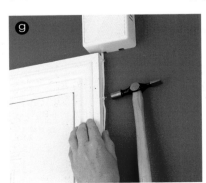

▶

Mending a fuse & fitting a plug

The job of mending a fuse is the great cliché of DIY – everybody is supposed to be able to mend a fuse! Seriously, the basic knowledge required for this job is an essential requirement of any responsible householder, as is fitting a plug.

▲ Locate the position of your fuse board, using a torch if necessary. Ensure that the master switch is in the OFF position and then find the individual fuse that needs its wire replacing.

The following is a very useful piece of information: always keep a torch, spare batteries, fuse wire, candles and matches as back-up in an accessible location close to the fuse board. This way, if you are plunged into darkness when a fuse blows, you will be fully prepared.

Mending a fuse

If your fuse board is in a dark and inaccessible location, as is often the case, use your torch to check that the fuse board master switch is in the OFF position. This will probably already be so, as when a fuse blows, normally it will automatically throw the master switch to the OFF position.

To locate the blown fuse, remove the fuses one at a time and inspect the thin fuse wire to make sure the wire is unbroken. On the card of fuse wire, select the appropriate amp fuse wire to match the blown fuse. Using a small screwdriver, carefully unscrew the two screws located a little way down at either end of the fuse. Remove the damaged remains of the old fuse wire and carefully thread the new wire through the centre porcelain part of the fuse. Wind the wire around the first screw, then the second, and tighten down the screws, snipping off any excess wire with a pair of wire cutters.

Replace the repaired fuse and then the fuse board cover. Throw the master switch to the ON position and power should be restored.

ELECTRICAL WORK

136

MUST KNOW

Tools required
Torch
Electrical screwdriver
Wire cutters
Ordinary screwdriver

Fitting a plug

Open up the plug case with a screwdriver and use wire strippers to remove the outer casing from each of the wires in the cable **[a]**. Use the ends of the wire cutters or a pair of pliers to position the exposed copper ends of each coloured wires in the correct terminals – brown to live, yellow and green to earth and blue to neutral **[b]**.

Holding the wires carefully in place in the terminals, drive the terminal screws tightly down on top of the wires using a screwdriver **[c]**. Finally, tighten up the screws securing the cable grip **[d]**, replace the plug cover and switch on.

WATCH OUT!

Watch the wires
When you secure the wires to the terminals in a plug, ensure that you do not leave any straggling ends of wire protruding.

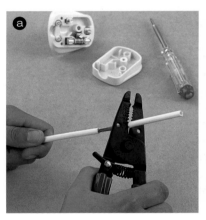

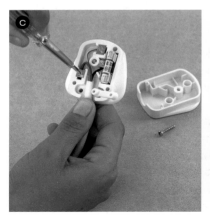

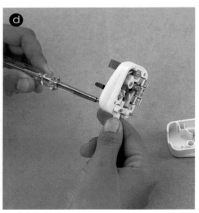

Changing a lightbulb holder

This is a useful skill to have if you wish to upgrade the fittings in a room, particularly after decorating, when old and dusty lightbulb holders can let down an otherwise pristine space.

Removing the old bulb holder

Before doing anything else, turn the power off! Then unscrew the top section of the bulb holder **[a]** to expose the two connecting wires. These wires will be held in place by two grub screws. Undo the two screws **[b]** to release the wires and remove the damaged bulb holder. The top part of the bulb holder will then slide down over the wires to complete the removal process.

The ends of the wires often become brittle from the heat of the bulb over a long period of time, so cut off the last inch (25mm) of flex. Then use the wire strippers to strip back the wire casing a further ½in (12mm) **[c]** before you fit the new bulb holder.

Sometimes, very old bulb holders can be difficult to unscrew. This is usually because ingrained dirt has got into the plastic threads. A little lubrication will normally solve the problem.

Fitting the new bulb holder

Unscrew the top section of the new bulb holder and slide this over the wires. Then, use a strip of tape **[d]** to hold the top section of the holder in place and stop it from sliding down, until you have connected the wires to the main body of the new bulb holder.

Undo the grub screws of the new bulb holder, insert the wires and tighten the grub

screws one at a time **[e]**. It does not matter
which side you put the wires into a bulb holder.
Loop them over the supporting lugs to prevent
the weight from being carried to the terminals
and to reduce stress on the unit as a whole.

Remove the tape to release the top part of
the bulb holder, and carefully screw it onto the
main body. Then unscrew the plastic retaining
ring which holds the lampshade in place, and
insert the shade **[f]**.

Carefully screw the retaining ring back on to
hold the lampshade in position **[g]**. Finally, insert
your new bulb, and turn the power back on.

If the new bulb holder will not work properly, it
is possible that either the bulb has blown or the
wiring is not properly secured. Check both.

MUST KNOW

Changing a bulb
Ascertain which kind of bulb you need – either
bayonet (push-in) or threaded (screw-in) – and
keep spares where you can find them easily. Turn
off the light switch (or the mains power
altogether, in the case of a faulty bulb holder).
Position a stepladder beneath the bulb holder.
Climb up and remove the lampshade if
necessary, prior to replacing the bulb. It is
normally secured by a threaded plastic ring.
Remove the old bulb by twisting or unscrewing
it and replace with the new bulb.

► Changing a socket

You might wish to change a socket as part of a general room makeover, perhaps after decorating, or to add extra practicality to a room by replacing a single socket with a double.

Before you begin this job, it's a good idea to plan where you think your furniture and appliances are going to be located around the room in question so that you can ensure that the power points are installed within easy reach. You may find that you need to move the socket from behind large furniture, or you want an extra power point without having to use an extension cable; these pages explain how you can do these things with minimum fuss.

Single power points are not much cheaper than doubles, so when fixing a new socket you might just as well fix a double.

The power supply is simply a continuous cable loop of 2.5mm twin and earth (three cores; two sheathed – live and neutral, one unsheathed – earth), pulled through where the power points are located, then looped on to the next point and so on. This is called a ring main. There is one on each floor of a house for power and a separate ring for lighting.

Changing from a single to a double power point

Turn OFF the power from the mains. Unscrew the retaining screws on the single socket face and pull the face out to reveal the cables **[a]**. Unscrew the wires and remove the socket face. Disconnect the interior of the single socket box and remove the back box by hand **[b]**.

If the power point is mounted in a plasterboard partition wall, mark the outline of the box on to the wall with a pencil and, using a

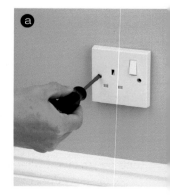

ⓐ

ELECTRICAL WORK

140

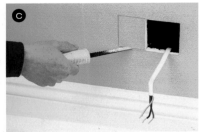

padsaw, cut out the piece of plasterboard **[c]**. Fix the new plasterboard back box, pulling the cables through to the front of the box **[d]**. The wiring will be the same for a single or double socket outlets – two red wires (live), two black (neutral) and two green and yellow (earth). Connect up the wires accordingly **[e]**, replace the double socket cover and secure the screws **[f]**.

If the power point is mounted in a solid wall, position the new double back box and mark the wall with a pencil. Remove the existing single socket box.

Using a masonry bit and drill, create a series of holes following your pencil line to the depth of the new back box. Then, use the club hammer and small bolster or cold chisel to break out the rest of the plaster and brickwork around the drilled holes.

Place the new double socket box in the new opening, mark two of the fixing holes. Using plugs and screws drill the holes, pull the cables through and fix the back-box in position, ensuring that it is flush with the plaster line. Finally, make good the edges of the opening around the box with filler and smooth with sandpaper. Re-decorate the area of wall around the socket as necessary.

ELECTRICAL WORK

Fitting wall lights

Wall lights offer an aesthetic and subtle alternative to overhead lights. It is important to think carefully about their positioning, but they are not especially difficult to install.

Cutting the chase

Mark where you want to position the wall lights, and using a spirit level and pencil, draw two vertical lines approx 40mm (1½in) wide up to the ceiling. Cut along the lines using a 1kg (2lb) club hammer and narrow bolster chisel. Using a cold chisel and hammer, cut back the plaster to form a chase or channel to house the cable **[a]**. Normally, the plaster is thick enough to house the cable, but it is good practice to house the cable in conduit or plastic capping to protect it. This may mean cutting the chase a little bit deeper to accommodate the conduit. Fixing the conduit or capping can be achieved by using 40mm (1½in) galvanized clout (plasterboard) nails knocked into the mortar joints **[b]**. Plaster

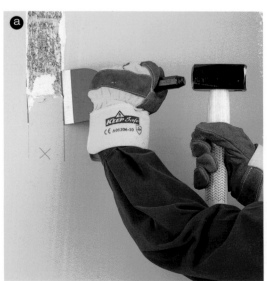

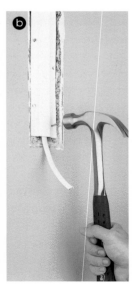

over the conduit to a smooth finish **[c]**. The cable you should use is the standard 1mm² twin and earth type. Fit the light switch and cable up to the junction box, and loop the cable in and out for each wall light mounting position, finishing the cable run at the last of the wall light mounting positions.

Cut back the ends of the conductors (wires), fixing the two red conductors into one terminal and the two black conductors into the second terminal. The earth wire should be sleeved and connected to the mounting box.

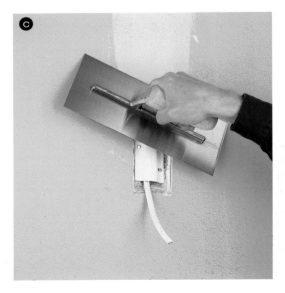

ⓒ

ELECTRICAL WORK

Fitting the wall light

Mark the fixing position of the wall lights on the wall with a spirit level and pencil **[d]**. If you are installing a sequence of wall lights across the wall – or on more than one wall of the room – ensure that they are both evenly spaced with one another and correctly centred on their particular section of the wall. Nothing looks worse than a pair or series of lights which are positioned out of kilter with one another.

Drill fixing holes into the wall for all the light fittings **[e]**, taking great care not to hit the cable in the chase as you do so. Insert rawlplugs into the wall and screw in hooks or screws by hand for securing the units to the

WATCH OUT!

Right circuit?
Ensure that you are absolutely clear exactly what you are wiring into what before embarking on this job. If in doubt, consult an electrician.

ELECTRICAL WORK

wall **[f]**. Hold up the wall light units, push the cable ends through the holes in the back and secure them to the wall **[g]**.

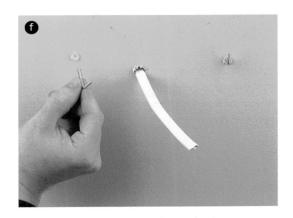

Cut back the rubber sheath protecting the conductors by about 12mm (½in) and fix the brown conductor into the other end of the red terminal and the blue conductor into the other end of the black terminal **[h]**. Make absolutely sure that you are putting the right wire into the right terminal before actually screwing the wire in place and making the connection.

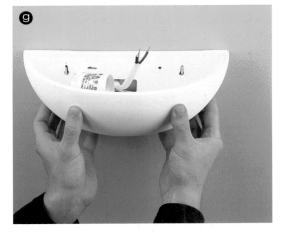

Always ensure that the mains power is turned OFF before making the final connection with the lighting ring main into the new junction box.

Turn the power on and enjoy the effect of your new wall lights. Finally, make good any damage to the room's decor caused by the installation of the lighting.

Fitting a spotlight track

A spotlight track offers another alternative form of lighting and is particularly useful for illuminating corners or dingy areas of the room. You can buy spotlight tracks as kits from many different outlets, and they come in numerous designs.

The connecting blocks of track systems are commonly positioned at one end of the track, so bear this in mind when making your choice, as it will affect where in the room you are able to locate the spotlights. There are also some tracks with the connection block situated in the middle of the track, which may save you having to make alterations to the lighting circuit.

Before you start, turn OFF the power. Unscrew the cover of the existing ceiling rose by hand **[a]** and then disconnect the wires from the terminals with an ordinary screwdriver **[b]**. Next, unscrew the base of the rose from the

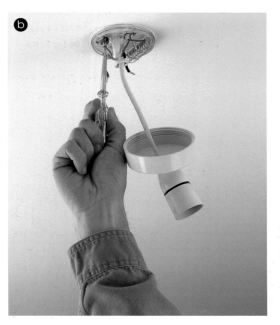

MUST KNOW

Tools required
Measuring tape
Electrical screwdriver
Hammer
Insulating tape
Nail bar
Ordinary screwdriver
Drill and pilot bit
Wire strippers

ceiling **[c]**. Assuming you have access to the floor above, lift the floorboard directly above the ceiling rose and replace the existing rose for a junction box located between the floorboards and the ceiling. Whenever possible, attach the track to some of the floor joists.

Mark drilling points with a pencil **[d]**, drill holes and press in rawlplugs to receive the screws

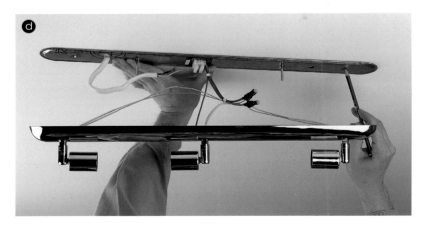

ELECTRICAL WORK

147

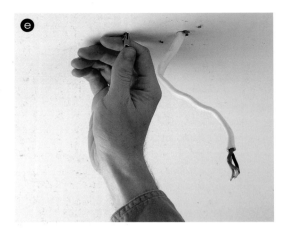

Low voltage lighting

Commonly known as 'downlighters', low voltage lighting systems provide an attractive feature but can be complicated to fit. However, there is a new, simpler low voltage system available without transformers, which are actually contained within the lamps. Check with your supplier whether conditions within your property are suitable for downlighters.

that will hold up the base of the track **[e]**. Alternatively, fix some battens above in the ceiling void to take the track fittings. Screw the base of the track to the joists or battens **[f]**, and then pull any excess flex into the ceiling void. Follow the instructions supplied with the track.

Wire one end of the length of flex into the junction box and the other end into the track connections **[g]**. Attach the cover of the spotlight track **[h]** and switch the power back on. Adjust the angles of the individual spotlights until they are illuminating different areas as appropriate. Avoid touching the spotlight bulbs.

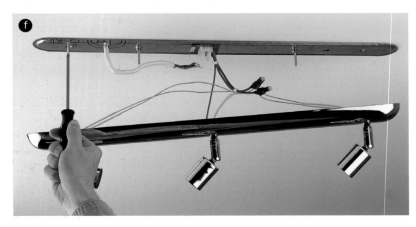

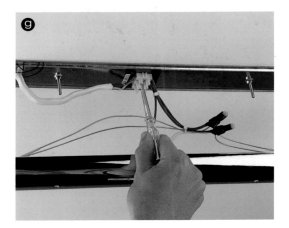

Ceiling fixings and instructions are normally supplied with all spotlight track systems. Remember to check that the number of lights you want to use will not overload the lighting circuit – the shop or DIY store where you buy the spotlight track should normally be able to advise you on this.

As a general rule, if you are in any doubt about performing an electrical task such as this one, don't do it – get a qualified electrician to come in instead. Electricity is one area of home DIY that you really cannot afford to take chances with...

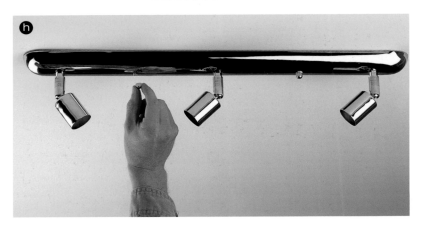

Fitting a decorative ceiling rose

Decorative ceiling roses were especially popular during the 19th century and are a feature of many Victorian houses. However, your house need not date from that period in order to benefit from one. Ceiling roses can be bought in ready-made packs and come in many different designs.

There are plenty of plaster ceiling roses to choose from. Plastic and polystyrene types are also widely available from DIY stores and good decorating shops. But if you want something special, you will need to go to a fibrous plaster specialist, who will offer a wide range of designs.

You may well manage to fix a small or medium-sized ceiling rose on your own or with the help of a partner, but for a large, heavy rose, it might be a good idea to enlist the help of friends, or bring in professional assistance.

Fitting a new ceiling rose

Make sure you set up a safe platform to work from before beginning work on the ceiling. Assuming you have no central light in place, the first thing to do is find the centre of the ceiling. This is achieved by using two lines of

MUST KNOW
Tools required
New ceiling rose
Tacks
String
Pencil
Straight edge
Joist detector
Drill
PVA adhesive
Brass screws
Screwdriver
Filler

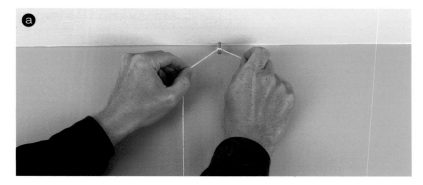

string each stretched diagonally from corner to corner of the ceiling **[a]**. The point where the strings cross each other will be the centre **[b]**. Where there is already a light fitting in place, remember to turn the power supply OFF and remove the fitting first.

Hold up the new ceiling rose (also centred) and draw around the edge with a pencil onto the ceiling to mark its fixing position **[c]**.

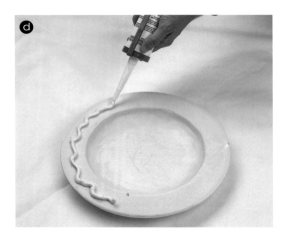

For a lightweight rose such as the one shown in the photographs, apply a coat of PVA adhesive and water to both the ceiling – removing any ceiling paper first – and the back of the rose to seal the surfaces **[d]**. Apply plaster or tile adhesive to the back of the rose and press it into place **[e]**. Wipe off any excess plaster or adhesive **[f]**. Ask someone to hold the rose in place and then pull the lighting flex through the centre of the rose. Use wire

WATCH OUT!

Fix it securely
Ensure that the fixing medium you select will take the weight of the rose you install, or your ceiling could be wrecked.

ELECTRICAL WORK

strippers to cut back the cable and strip the
wires ready for wiring into the light fitting [g].
Fill over any screwheads with filler and leave to
dry. Paint to finish, tying the rose carefully into
the ceiling.

If you wish to install a particularly heavy ceiling
rose, use a joist detector to locate the joists
within the proximity of the rose. Take the
straight edge and pencil and draw two centre
lines on the ceiling and transfer corresponding
lines onto the rose. Carefully drill two pilot holes,
then a light countersink and have two long
brass screws ready for fixing.

want to know more?

Take it to the next level...

Go to...
► Electrical tools – page 10
► Security lighting – pages 182–5
► Electrical regulations – page 189

Other sources
► **Local authority building control**
www.labc-services.co.uk
► **Other electrical projects**
visit www.diydoctor.org.uk for advice
► **Finding a skilled electrician**
Visit the site of the National Inspection
Council for Electrical Installation
Contracting (NICEIC) www.niceic.org.uk
► **Electricity safety tips**
www.niceic.org.uk/consumers/tips.html

outdoor

jobs

One of the best things about learning DIY skills is that you can improve not only your house but your garden, driveway, paths, outbuildings and any number of other outdoor features as well. Here is a selection of popular outdoor DIY jobs and projects.

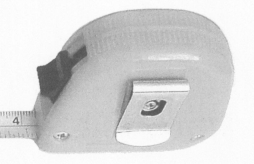

Repairing/ re-aligning a gate

Garden gates become damaged and gradually break down with constant use, so a common repair is hinge or catch re-alignment. Wooden gates in particular tend to rot in poor weather, so that general repairs are also sometimes called for.

The main problem with ageing gates is that as they get older they begin to sag on their hinges, no longer aligning with the gate catch on the post. To re-align the catch, use a drill to create pilot holes for re-fixing **[a]** and simply re-locate the striking plate on the gatepost, securing it with wood screws.

Timber shrinks as it dries out, so a good tip is to use slightly longer screws to create a firm fixing **[b]**, in order that the striking plate does not slip once more on the post.

If the gate has a number of rotten sections in it, lay the gate on a pair of stools or a work bench before working on it. Carefully remove the offending

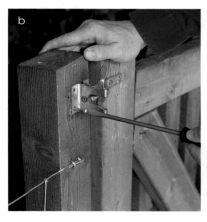

MUST KNOW

Tools required
Cordless drill
Screwdriver
Saw
Jigsaw
Claw hammer
Pinchers
Paintbrush
Sandpaper

rotten pieces, using a claw hammer, pinchers, a screwdriver or whichever tool seems the most appropriate **[c]**.

Using an existing section of the gate as a template, cut and shape a replacement piece of new timber **[d]**. Ensure that the replacement timber has a good few coats of preservative **[e]**, and two as an absolute minimum, before fixing the new section to the gate.

Pilot drill and countersink the fixing screws for the new picket or replacement section **[f]**. Fill over the screw heads, sandpaper the whole gate down thoroughly and re-coat it with preservative, not forgetting to paint the gate posts as well.

If you choose paint instead of wood

preservative for your gate, be warned that it will not protect the gate as thoroughly and this means that the life of your gate is likely to be foreshortened by rot or blistering. Before painting, ensure that any bare wood is properly primed, and then apply a minimum of two undercoats and one topcoat. When you are satisfied, re-hang the gate **[g]**, ensuring that it clears the path and aligns perfectly with its posts.

Repairing a fence

If your garden fence rots or blows down in high wind, it can be very expensive to have it repaired professionally. It is so much better to have the skills to prevent such problems from occurring in the first place, and keep the fence upright.

There are basically two types of common fence. The first is the gravel board variety (named after the bit of the fence in contact with the soil), which will not rot and is used in conjunction with concrete posts and wooden panels. Although maintenance-free, this type of fence is rather conspicuous and not especially good-looking. The second common type of fence is made completely of wood – preferably pressure-treated. When the bottom gravel board panels rot, they can be simply replaced with new pieces by means of a couple of screws at either end into the base of the post **[a]**.

Most timber fencing products come pre-coated in brown wooden preservative, or a slightly more ambitious golden brown colour, which tends to fade quickly as it is only a water-based dip solution. It is a good idea to apply your own preservative coating over the top of these basic, generally cheap preparations. A huge selection of both water- and spirit-based

OUTDOOR JOBS

158

wood preservatives is now available in an amazing range of colours.

The job of erecting a new post is relatively straightforward once you have removed the remains of the old one. The new post requires a hole that is a minimum depth of 460mm (18in). Use a stiff concrete mix dry or with not too much water – it should be the consistency of double cream. Pack the concrete in around the post with a wooden batten **[c]**.

Ensure that the post is level on two adjoining sides, and aligned with the other posts by use of a string line. Attach some temporary braces to keep the post upright whilst the concrete sets **[d]**.

Obviously, softwood posts only last so long in the soil. To increase the post life, use pressure-treated posts. Alternatively stand the posts upright in a bucket of preservative for a minimum of two days, to help extend the lifespan of the post **[e]**.

One alternative way to fix posts, which offers the advantage of avoiding digging, is to use metpost spikes. These can be a useful alternative to concreting. It is essential to knock them in straight, using the resin block supplied, with the firm swing of a sledgehammer **[f]**. Once the metpost is firmly in the ground, simply slip the end of the fence post into it **[g]**.

OUTDOOR JOBS

Making & erecting trellis

A new garden trellis can double both as a beautiful garden feature and as a practical innovation offering support and protection to a wide variety of plants. Trellis is available in a variety of pre-made styles and is not difficult to erect.

People often want to increase the height of an existing boundary. A simple and attractive method of achieving this without breaking the bank is to add a trellis. Not only will the trellis add height to the boundary and reduce exposure to the gaze of neighbours or passers-by, if well planted it will soon become a major focal point in most gardens.

To fix a post to a wall, first cut the post to half its width using a sharp saw – a minimum distance of 610mm (2ft) up from the bottom of the post. After treating the exposed cut surface with a good quality wood preservative **[a]**, drill pilot holes through the post and attach it to the wall with frame fixings or plugs and screws **[b]**. Run a string line between all the posts as you erect them, in order to ensure that they are all

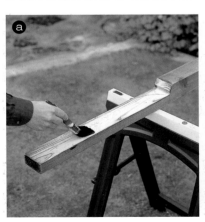

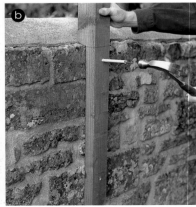

Getting things straight

Never attach or set your trellis posts until you
are certain they are positioned perfectly in line
with one another and at the same height. Good
trellis building is all in the preparation – like so
many DIY jobs – and a crooked or uneven trellis
will haunt you every time you look at it, so take
your time to get it right.

correctly aligned along the boundary. Use thin
packers of wood offcuts or cardboard to adjust
the posts to suit the spirit level and string line,
until they are perfectly level and in true with one
another. Next, simply pilot drill and screw fix the
trellis panels to the posts **[c]**. Purchase – or
make and fix – flat post caps, to protect the
post end grain from the weather.

   If you are ambitious, you could make the trellis
panels yourself. A really simple and good-
looking trellis to make is the diamond pattern.

   Once the panel size has been decided
(remember, you are no longer restricted to
standard size panels), make an outside frame
and simply nail the components together using
ring nails **[d]**. These nails have a type of thread

which prevents the panel from parting from the post – a particularly useful feature if your garden is prone to high winds!

Set a 45° angle with the adjustable square, and then mark the frame and nail on the first batten. Using equal spacers top and bottom, set out and fix the next batten **[e]**, ensuring that it sits perfectly in line with the first batten before you attach it to the frame. Repeat this process across the frame. Again using the adjustable square, reverse the pattern using the same spacers, fixing the battens across the first layer of battens. Once again, use ring nails to attach these battens.

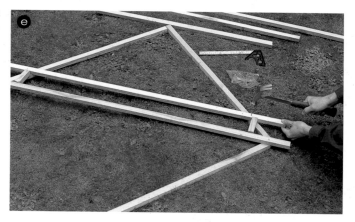

Think about your plants

If you intend to design and build your own trellis, rather than buying one ready-made, it might be a good idea to think about what you propose growing up it once it is completed. For example, if you create a trellis with a gappy, large pattern, it won't necessarily be suitable for plants that require a lot of close support when they are first becoming established. By the same token, an ornate, intricately patterned trellis might be wasted behind an invasive climbing plant with a dense spreading habit. Another consideration is to only ever paint trellis with plant-friendly substances, as some paints can be poisonous.

When you have attached all the battens and completed the pattern of diamonds across the entire frame, trim off the excess timber to form a neat, consistent panel **[g]**. Finally, decorate the panel to your taste.

To make a square trellis, use exactly the same method as described above but instead apply the spacers at a 90° angle to each layer rather than the 45° angle that forms the diamonds **[h]**. Remember that the length of the spacers determines the size of the squares.

Patio repairs

Like all outdoor features, patios are prone to wear and tear and the vagaries of the weather. No matter how durable the materials of your patio might be, at some point you will need to make basic repairs or improvements.

Patios in north-facing gardens are particularly prone to problems, as algae and lichen flourish in the damp conditions of these gardens. Here are a few pointers as to how to keep your patio in the best possible condition.

Paving slabs should be laid on a mortar bed, NEVER on sand. If they have been laid on sand, pick them up, clean them off and re-lay them on a mortar bed. Do not try to economise by only 'spotting' the mortar, or you will be overrun with insects in no time. Instead, lay the slabs on a full mortar bed for paving – four parts sharp sand, two parts soft sand, one part cement. Use a bucket to gauge the materials accurately. Make the mix wet by adding water and keep it pliable by adding plasticiser to the mix.

If your patio has been well-laid but has become dirty, or algae covered, remove the algae by using an acid patio cleaner. There are various good

MUST KNOW
Tools required
Club hammer
Small bolster chisel
Cold chisel
Shovel
Yard broom
Soft brush
Watering can
Mixing board/mixer
Trowel
Jointer

a

proprietary brands. Follow the instructions carefully and wear protective clothing. Mix the chemical with water and apply with a watering can **[a]**, vigorously rub over the surface with a yard broom and rinse with cold water.

If your patio has been laid on sand, and weeds are growing up through it, rake out the weeds and debris using a trowel and chisel **[b]**, sweep off and re-point the gaps between the slabs. Re-point using a mixture of three parts dry soft sand to one part cement. Sweep into the joints **[c]**, and rub over the joints with a jointer.

To replace a damaged slab, rake out the old jointing using a cold chisel and club hammer **[d]**,

and then break out the damaged slab with a crowbar, levering it against an offcut of wood to prevent damage to the neighbouring slab **[e]**. Next, re-bed the replacement slab **[f]**. You can use dry mortar sprinkled into the hole, then wet it down with a watering can before the slab is laid, although ideally you should use wet mortar to ensure better adhesion and lessen the likelihood of weeds emerging from underneath the replacement slab.

Ensure that the replacement slab is level with the surrounding paving by tapping it down so that the level matches perfectly all round. Use a rubber mallet, or the wooden handle of a club hammer, to gently tap the slab into place **[g]**, taking great care to ensure that you do not break the

WATCH OUT!

On the level
Do not put too much mortar into the space vacated by the broken slab. Once the new slab goes in, it will be hard to remove again.

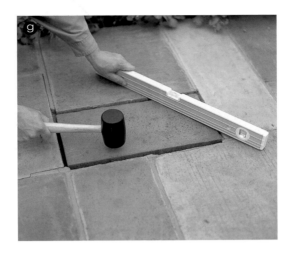

slab in the process. All that remains to be done is the pointing **[h]**, using exactly the same technique as described earlier.

When pointing replacement slabs, try to ensure that you use exactly the same mixture for the grout as you did when you first laid the patio, as otherwise the new grout will dry to a different colour and the replacement slab will stand out. Weathering takes care of this problem in time, but the less obtrusive any repairs are at the outset, the better.

Building a barbecue

You can buy barbecues in every conceivable shape and size from any number of different outlets, but if you are serious about barbecuing and enjoy your DIY, what could be more satisfying than building your own? The materials that make up this barbecue are relatively expensive, but it will last for years.

The site chosen for this barbecue was a paved utility area, to the side of the main patio. The garden was large, so the barbecue didn't suddenly become the dominant feature. Wherever you decide to build your barbecue, it must be on a solid hardstand (a bit of concrete or paving).

Make a wooden frame to act as a template guide to the dimensions of the grill kit. Lay the bricks out dry (without mortar) to enable the correct brickwork bond to be determined. Bed the bricks on a bed of mortar made up of five parts soft building sand to one part cement, with plasticiser added to keep the mix supple [a].

Use a spirit level to ensure the brickwork is level and plumb. Here, a paving slab is being

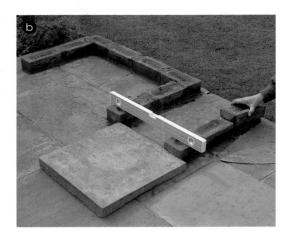

used to act as a tabletop. Lay the slab down as a guide to the independent leg position **[b]**. You can use either a 1 x 0.6m (3 x 2ft) paving slab, or a 0.6 x 0.6m (2 x 2ft) slab like this one.

To get the brickwork bond correct, it is necessary to cut half bricks. Cut these on a soft surface with a bolster chisel and club hammer **[c]**. Wear protective clothing for this operation.

When you have built the brickwork to the correct height for the slab table, turn some of the bricks as shown **[d]**, so that they act as

WATCH OUT!

Keep it level
Use your spirit level throughout the build to ensure that everything is level. This will reduce cooking disasters later on!

corbels (supports) for the table and the grate. Ensure that you measure the width of the grate accurately before finally placing and securing the corbels so that you will be sure of a good fit once the grate is in place in the finished barbecue.

Repeat the corbels two courses up to support the cooking griddle **[e]**. Again, measure the position of these carfeully to ensure that there are no unpleasant surprises once the barbecue is complete.

Two more courses of bricks are required to complete the barbecue. Push four metal pins into the mortar below the top course of brickwork to support the warming griddle shelf **[f]**.

You might want to fit a decorative flat coping or brick-on-edge course to finish off. Not only will this look good, it will also usefully serve as a rest for drinks during cooking.

Set the paving slab on a bed of mortar to make a table top alongside the main body of the barbecue **[g]**. Leave the brickwork to cure for a couple of hours. Then, using a jointer (a bent copper pipe or garden hose will suffice if you do not have the actual tool), rake out the top crust of the mortar, to make a tidy job.

Finally, take a soft hand brush and carefully brush over the brickwork to complete the job **[h]**, ensuring that you do not disturb the mortar.

Erecting a shed

Garden sheds of many different sizes can be bought from garden centres and DIY stores. They normally come with full manufacturer's instructions and are not difficult to assemble.

A concrete screed is often the preferred base for a garden shed, but that can be a laborious and expensive way to create a base. If the shed has a wooden floor, as most of them do, ideally the structure should be slightly elevated off the ground to allow air to circulate underneath, as this prevents rot from setting in. The following is a quick, cheap and simple method of creating a shed base support system.

Cut three concrete or breeze blocks (but not lightweight blocks), in half to form six pads. Position these at the four corners of the wooden floor section and two centrally beneath it. Using a spade, dig the pads in so the blocks remain just above the surface. Adjust the pads by packing or excavating to ensure that they are all level, using a spirit level and board. Simply place the 100 x 100mm (4 x 4in) pressure-treated posts across the pads as bearers for the floor section **[a]**.

Lay the floor section across the bearers **[b]** (no fixings are required for this part of the assembly), and double-check for level.

MUST KNOW

Tools required
Spade
Spirit level
Hammer
Cordless
    drill/screwdriver
Tape measure

Fit the walls next. If you don't have anyone to help you, support the first panel in place with an angled prop, while you screw fix through the bottom rail into the base. Position the second section and screw fix through the side rail **[c]**, then do the same through the base rail and remove the prop. Simply attach the remaining panels in the same way. The roof is normally made into easy-fit sections, which slot into a rebate **[d]**. Screw fix through the rails to secure.

The felt is normally fixed in three sections, with the central ridge piece being fixed last over the two side sections and nailed down with galvanised clout nails to secure the felt **[e]**. This method ensures a waterproof lap, so take care not to damage the felt during construction.

Fascia boards are fitted to the front and rear elevations to keep the felt in place. The felt can be simply nailed with clout nails on either side, or turned under and fixed with a timber batten along its length (on the underside).You can attach a finial at either end to cover the fascia joints **[f]**, with corner trims nailed to the four vertical corners to finish the job.

Replacing the felt on a shed roof

Bitumen felt is commonly used for protecting the roofs of wooden sheds. While it is an inexpensive and effective form of weatherproofing, it wears out quite quickly and needs replacing.

Begin by removing the nails from the timber **[a]** and stripping off the old roof covering **[b]**. Make sure that you wear safety goggles and gloves when you are doing this. At the same time, you could take the opportunity to apply a coat of preservative to the exposed timber roof panels.

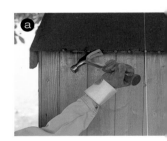

Unroll the felt, measure the length required, and then mark and cut it with a craft knife and straightedge **[c]**. Always allow at least a couple of inches overhang at either end. Roll the cut lengths up again and roll out onto each side of the roof in turn **[d]**, allowing an inch or two of overhang. Nail the felt along the ridge edge with galvanised clout nails to secure it **[e]**. Repeat on the other side.

Cut the third section to size, allowing a minimum overlap of 50mm (2in) either side. This is called the ridge-capping piece. The ridge

Tools required
Nail bar
Claw hammer
Pinchers
Scraper
Craft knife
Mastic gun
Straight edge
Safety glasses
Protective gloves

piece can be attached with clout nails or a mastic sealer adhesive. Apply the mastic beads with a mastic gun **[f]**. Roll out the felt and press it into place, working from the middle outwards **[g]**. Finally, nail all around the overhung edges to secure the felt covering from blowing off in the wind **[h]**.

You can give shed roof felt a longer lease of life by periodically painting it with a bitumen paint. This is thick and sticky to apply, but will save you having to replace the roof felt as frequently. Bitumen paint is widely available at DIY stores.

Installing an external water tap

There is always a need for running water outside, but often no external water tap to supply it. Perhaps surprisingly, fitting one yourself is actually quite an easy and hassle-free job.

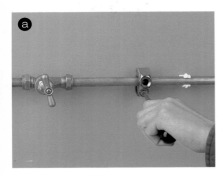

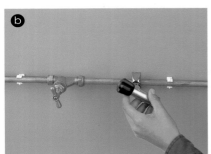

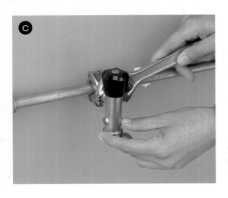

Conventional ways of fitting an external tap usually consist of installing a 'Tee joint' in the mains supply, and running a copper pipe through the wall to an external tap known as a 'bibcock'. There are various different ways of installing an external water tap, especially since the introduction of plastic water pipes. Here, we demonstrate just one way of installing an outside tap quickly and easily.

The first step is to fit a connection to the existing cold feed line on the non-pressure side of the stop valve. You can do this by fitting a self-bore valve. This will make a hole in the pipe without you having to turn off the water, which can save inconvenience.

Place the saddle over the pipe and screw this onto the back plate. This will firmly fix it over the pipe ready for the valve **[a]**.

Now slowly but firmly screw in the valve **[b]**, making sure beforehand that it is in the OFF position. Insert the valve until you are sure you have made a hole in the pipe, keeping the valve in the vertical position with the outlet down. Using an adjustable spanner, tighten up the lock nut on the valve onto the saddle to secure a watertight joint **[c]**. Now screw on the hose to the valve outlet **[d]**.

Using your hammer drill and bit, drill a hole in the external wall from the inside out, checking its location both inside and out to make sure it arrives where you want it. It is important to

ensure that the hole does not appear in an awkward or conspicuous place. Now pass the flexible hose through the wall **[e]**. Next, you will need to fix the tap back plate onto the wall, vertically in line with the hose about 150–200mm (6–8in) below the hole. Having drilled a hole for the back plate screw, fix your screw to the wall using a wall plug of a suitable size and then screw the tap back plate to this. Install the tap in a vertical position with the inlet for the hose connector pointing up. Fit a jubilee clip over the hose and the hose over the male side of the connector. Tighten the jubilee clip for a watertight connection **[f]**, but not so tight as to cut into the hose. Now screw the female connector onto the male tap connector and tighten the joint as firmly as you can with your fingers **[g]**. Finally, screw on the body of the tap **[h]**.

Each winter, remember to isolate the outside tap against freezing by turning the inside tap to the OFF position and the outside tap to the ON position, to drain off any residue.

OUTDOOR JOBS

Installing an external power source

Much in the same way as a source of external water is very useful, so is an external source of electricity. The usual caveats about working with electricity apply here – that is, if you are not sure don't do it – but the job is relatively straightforward.

A wide range of outdoor power sockets are available for sale. The type demonstrated here is good quality and water-resistant with a built in RCD (residual current device), which in simple terms means to say that the device will cut out and isolate any appliance attached to it in the event of rain, a power surge or any other potentially life-threatening event. To connect it, ideally run 2.5mm twin and earth cable from the external socket through the wall to the consumer unit. Alternatively, you could add to the existing power ring main, or simply add a spur from an existing socket to provide the power source.

Drill through the wall with a suitable masonry bit and hammer drill. Feed through the 2.5mm

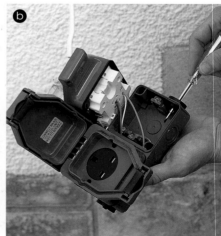

Tools required
Masonry drill and bits
Hammer
Electrical screwdriver
Screwdriver
  or cordless driver
Cable stripper

OUTDOOR JOBS

179

twin and earth cable, but do not connect to the
ring main until after fitting the external socket.

Unscrew the switch face **[a]** and lift out to
reveal the cable connection terminals **[b]**. Feed
the cable through the protective rubber flange.
Position the socket in place, and mark the fixing
points. Using a masonry drill to create the holes,
fix the socket with plugs and screws **[c]**.

WATCH OUT!

Take precautions

If in any doubt about your ability to do this job, do not take it on – hire a professional electrician instead. Refer to the electrical work safety tips given in Chapter 6 of this book and observe the following basic precautions: always turn off the power before beginning any electrical work; NEVER work in the rain or when the ground is very wet; check all electrical connections carefully.

Use cable strippers to reveal the wire conductors **[d]** (see page 179) and connect the conductors to the appropriate terminals: red = live; black = neutral; yellow and green = earth **[e]**.

Screw back the socket face **[f]**, and make the internal connections to the power supply (as covered in Changing Sockets, see pages 140–1). Finally, switch on the power supply, plug in the outdoor appliance you wish to use **[g]**, close the cover **[h]** and make sure that everything is working as it should.

security light to suit your personal requirements
[g]. This is normally easily done by turning a
knob with your fingers or a screwdriver. Refer to
the manufacturer's instructions of the light in
question.

Individual sensors can be prepared and
installed independently of the light fitting, to
enlarge the catchment area or to create an
early warning system **[h]**.

want to know **more?**

Take it to the next level...

Go to...
▶ **Planning the job** – pages 18–19
▶ **Varnishing windows** – pages 32–33
▶ **Spotlight track** – pages 146–9

Other sources
▶ **Local DIY stores**
   can usually offer plenty of advice if you
   are unsure about tackling a job
▶ **DIY courses**
   check with your local authority for adult
   evening classes in practical woodwork
▶ **Manufacturer's booklets**
   product leaflets can offer inspiration
▶ **Internet websites**
   visit www.diynot.com

Glossary

Airlock: A blockage in a pipe caused by a trapped bubble of air.

Appliance: A machine or device powered by electricity.

Architrave: The moulding around a window or door.

Back siphoning: The siphoning of part of a plumbing system caused by the failure of mains water pressure.

Baluster: One of a set of posts supporting a stair handrail.

Balustrade: The protective barrier alongside a staircase or landing.

Basecoat: A flat coat of paint over which a decorative glaze is applied.

Batt: A short cut length of glass-fibre or mineral-fibre insulant.

Batten: A narrow strip of wood.

Bore: The hollow part of a pipe.

Cap-nut: The nut used to tighten a fitting onto pipework.

Casing: The timber lining of a door or window opening.

Cavity wall: A wall made of two separate, parallel masonry skins with an air space between them.

Chamfer: A narrow flat surface along the edge of a workpiece – normally at an angle of 45° to adjacent surfaces.

Chase: A groove cut in masonry or plaster to accept pipework or an electrical cable; or to cut or channel such grooves.

Circuit: A complete path through which an electric current can flow.

Concave: Curving inwards.

Conductor: A component, usually a length of wire, along which an electric current will pass.

Convex: Curving outwards.

Cornice: Continuous horizontal moulding between the walls and ceiling of a room.

Counterbore: To cut a hole that allows the head of a bolt or screw to lie below a surface.

Countersink: To cut a tapered recess that allows the head of a screw to be flush with a surface; or the tapered recess itself.

Coving: A prefabricated moulding used to make a cornice.

Cup: To bend as a result of shrinkage, specifically across the width of a piece of wood.

Dado: The lower part of an interior wall – usually defined by a moulded wooden rail at about waist height (the dado rail).

Damp-proof course: A layer of impervious material that prevents moisture rising through a concrete floor.

Drop: A strip of wallpaper measured and cut to length ready for pasting to a wall.

Earth: A connection between an electrical circuit and the earth (ground); or a terminal to which the connection is made.

Eaves: The edges of a roof that project beyond the walls.

Extension: A room or rooms added to an existing building.

Extension lead: A length of electrical flex for temporarily connecting the short permanent flex of an appliance to a wall socket.

Face edge: In woodworking, the surface which is planed square to the face side of the piece of work.

Face side: In woodworking, the flat planed surface from which other dimensions and angles are measured and worked.

Fascia: A strip of wood that covers the ends of rafters and to which external guttering is fixed.

Feather: To wear away or smooth an edge until it is undetectable.

Fence: An adjustable guide to keep the cutting edge of a tool a set distance from the edge of a workpiece.

Fuse board: Where the main electrical service cable is connected to the house circuitry; or the accumulation of consumer unit, meter, etc.

Galvanized: Covered with a protective coating of zinc.

Grain: The general direction of wood fibres; or the pattern produced on the surface of timber by cutting through the fibres.

Groove: A long narrow channel cut in plaster or wood in the general direction of the grain.

Grounds: Strips of wood fixed to a wall to

provide nail-fixing points for skirting boards, door casings, etc.

Head plate: The top horizontal member of a stud partition.

Housing: A long narrow channel cut across the general direction of wood grain to form part of a joint.

Insulation: Materials used to reduce the transmission of heat or sound; or nonconductive material surrounding electrical wires or connections to prevent the passage of electricity.

Jamb: The vertical side of a doorframe or window frame.

Joist: A horizontal wooden or metal beam (such as an RSJ) used to support a structure such as a floor, ceiling or wall.

Key: To abrade a surface in order to provide a better grip when gluing something to it.

Knotting: Sealer, made from shellac, that prevents wood resin bleeding through a surface finish.

Knurled: Impressed with a series of fine grooves designed to improve the grip, for instance a knurled knob or handle on a tool.

Lintel: A horizontal beam used to support the wall over a door or window opening.

Mastic: A nonsetting compound used to seal joints.

Mitre: A joint formed between two pieces of wood by cutting bevels of equal angle at the ends of each piece; or to cut the joint.

Pallet: A wooden plug built into masonry to provide a fixing point for a door casing.

Pilot hole: A small-diameter hole drilled prior to the insertion of a woodscrew to act as a guide for its thread.

Primer: The first coat of a paint system applied to protect wood or metal.

Profile: The outline or contour of an object.

PTFE: Polytetrafluorethylene – a material used to make tape for sealing threaded plumbing fittings.

Purlin: A horizontal beam that provides intermediate support for rafters or sheet roofing.

Rafter: One of a set of parallel sloping beams that form the main structural element of a roof.

Rebate: A stepped rectangular recess along the edge of a workpiece, usually forming part of a joint; or to cut such recesses.

Residual current device: A device that monitors the flow of electrical current through the live and neutral wires of a circuit.

Reveal: The vertical side of an opening.

Riser: The vertical part of a step.

Rising main: The pipe that supplies water under mains pressure, usually to a storage tank in the roof.

Rolled steel joist (RSJ): A steel beam, usually with a cross section in the form of a capital letter I.

Sash: The openable part of a window.

Score: To scratch a line with a pointed tool.

Scribe: To copy the profile of a surface on the edge of sheet material that is to be butted against it; or to mark a line with a pointed tool.

Sheathing: The outer layer of insulation on an electrical cable or flex.

Short circuit: The accidental re-routing of electricity to earth, which increases the flow of current and eventually blows a fuse.

Stud partition: A timber frame interior dividing wall.

Studs: The vertical members of a timber frame wall.

Tamp: To pack down firmly with repeated blows.

Template: A cut-out pattern made from paper, wood, metal, etc, to help shape a workpiece accurately.

Terminal: A connection to which the bared ends of electrical cable or flex are attached.

Thinner: A solvent, such as turpentine, used to dilute paint or varnish.

Trap: A bent section of pipe below a bath, sink, etc. It contains standing water to prevent the passage of gases.

Tread: The horizontal part of a step.

Undercoat: A layer or layers of paint used to obliterate the colour of a primer and build up a protective body of paint before the top coat is applied.

Need to know more?

Listed below are just some of the websites, books and magazines available to aid you further in your DIY knowledge, as well as a few professional organisations which you can trust to help you if you get in a fix.

Useful website addresses
www.bbc.co.uk/homes/diy
www.diyfixit.co.uk
www.diy.com
www.decoratingdirect.co.uk
www.thehouseplanner.co.uk
www.askthebuilder.com
www.diydoctor.org.uk
www.niceic.org.uk/consumers/
    tips.html
www.diynot.com

Magazines
Home DIY (published by Highbury
    Leisure)
House Beautiful (published by The
    National magazine Company)
Practical Woodworking (published
    by Highbury–Nexus)
The English Home (published by
    The Magazine Group)

Bibliography
The DIY Manual, HarperCollins,
ISBN 0 00 718523 5
Tommy Walsh Bathroom DIY,
HarperCollins, 0 00 715689 8
Tommy Walsh Kitchen DIY,
HarperCollins, 0 00 715688 X

Tommy Walsh Living Spaces DIY,
HarperCollins, 0 00 715686 3
Tommy Walsh Outdoor DIY,
HarperCollins, 0 00 715687 1
Fix It Manual, HarperCollins,
0 00 412993 8
*The Complete Guide to Home
Carpentry*, Creative Publishing
International, 0 86 573577 8
Plumbing Basics, Meredith Books,
0 89 721439 0

Organisations
The Institute of Plumbing and
Heating Engineering (IPHE).
Visit the website for registered
plumbers: **www.iphe.org.uk**

The National Inspection Council for
Electrical Installation Contracting
(NICEIC) provides a list of qualified
electricians: **www.niceic.org.uk**

Visit **www.qualitymark.org.uk**
to find a reputable and
trustworthy tradesman in your
area who is a member of the
government-backed Quality
Mark Scheme.

New regulations

From spring 2005, there are new government regulations that stipulate all domestic electrical installations – with the exception of minor work – must now be inspected by a 'competent' or certified person.

In practice, this means that certain projects that you were once able to carry out in a home DIY capacity will now need to be checked. Jobs such as installing a power shower or a cooker, rewiring or replacing damaged circuits, installing a pond pump in the garden and putting in electrical installations in the shed or garage will need to be inspected by a qualified electrician or the local authority building control department.

DIY-ers will still be able to replace socket outlets, control switches and ceiling roses without needing to be inspected. However, the rules are complex and it is best to consult any of the following if you are at all unclear as to what is and what is not allowed.

- For details of exceptions to the new rules, visit **www.partp.co.uk** or **www.odpm.gov.uk**
- For technical inquiries, contact the building regulations division of the ODPM (Office of the Deputy Prime Minister) 020 7944 5734 energy.br@odpm.gsi.gov.uk
- Local authority building control 020 7641 8737 (website listings for your local division) **www.labc-services.co.uk**
- Electrical Contractors' Association (for certified electricians) 020 7313 4800 **www.eca.co.uk**
- National Inspection Council for Electrical Installation Contracting (to find an electrician) 020 7564 2323 **www.niceic.org.uk**
- Institute of Electrical Engineers 020 7240 1871 **www.iee.org**
- The Quality Mark Scheme, a government-backed site for traders by postcode, and for checks: **www.qualitymark.org.uk**

Index

need to know?

Want to know about other popular subjects and activities? Look out for further titles in Collins' practical and accessible **Need to Know?** series.

Digital photography
All the kit, techniques and tips you need to take great photographs

192pp   £8.99
PB   0 00 718031 4

Golf
All the kit, techniques and inspiration to get into the game

192pp   £8.99
PB   0 00 718037 3

Zodiac types
Yourself, your friends and your family revealed

192pp   £7.99
PB   0 00 718038 1

Watercolour
All the kit, techniques and inspiration you need to get into painting

192pp   £8.99
PB   0 00 718032

Card games
All the rules and tips you need to start playing over 60 card games

192pp   £6.99
PB   0 00 719080 8

Yoga
All the tips and techniques you need to get healthy in mind and body

192pp   £8.99
PB   0 00 719091 3

Pilates
All the tips and techniques you need to get a lithe, flexible body

192pp   £8.99
PB   0 00 719063 8

Guitar
All the gear, techniques and tips you need to play the guitar

192pp   £9.99
PB   0 00 719088

DIY
All the know-how you need to get doing it yourself

192pp   £8.99
PB   0 00 719447 1

Weddings
All the facts, advice and inspiration you need for the perfect wedding

208pp   £9.99
PB   0 00 719703 9

Drawing & Sketching
All the techniques and inspiration you need to start drawing

192pp   £8.99
PB   0 00 719327 0

Birdwatching
All the tips and techniques you need to get into birdwatching

192pp   £8.99
PB   0 00 719527

Forthcoming titles:

Stargazing
Kama Sutra
Dog Training
Knots
The World

How to Lose Weight
Sleep
Detox
Food Allergies
Wine

To order any of these titles, please telephone **0870 787 1732**. For further information about all Collins books, visit our website: **www.collins.co.uk**

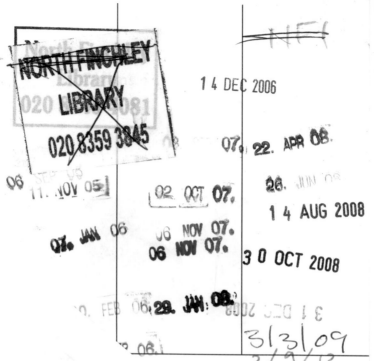